ROMAN PROVENCE

Other non-fiction by Edwin Mullins includes
  Braque
  Alfred Wallis
  A Love Affair with Nature
  The Arts of Britain
  The Painted Witch

And published by Signal Books –
  The Pilgrimage to Santiago
  In Search of Cluny
  Avignon of the Popes
  The Camargue

(www.signalbooks.co.uk)

ROMAN PROVENCE
A History and Guide

Edwin Mullins

Signal Books
Oxford

First published in 2011 by
Signal Books Limited
36 Minster Road
Oxford
OX4 1LY
www.signalbooks.co.uk

© Edwin Mullins, 2011

The right of Edwin Mullins to be identified as the author of this work has been asserted by him in accordance with the Copyright, Design and Patents Act, 1988.

All rights reserved. The whole of this work, including all text and illustrations, is protected by copyright. No parts of this work may be loaded, stored, manipulated, reproduced or transmitted in any form or by any means, electronic or mechanical, including photocopying and recording, or by any information, storage and retrieval system without prior written permission from the publisher, on behalf of the copyright owner.

A catalogue record for this book is available from the British Library.

ISBN 978-1-904955-91-7 Paper

Production: Devdan Sen
Cover Design: Devdan Sen
Cover Images: Library of Congress; Wikipedia Commons
Illustrations: Library of Congress; Wikipedia Commons
Printed by Short Run Press Ltd, Exeter, UK

CONTENTS

Author's Preface   vii

1.
The Eagle Spreads its Wings   1
Les Baux-de-Provence: *Les Tremaïe*   13

2.
Caesar and Caesar   19
La Turbie: the Trophée des Alpes   34

3.
Triumph and Triumphalism   37
St.-Rémy de Provence: the Triumphal Arch   46

4.
The Architecture of Water   53
The Pont du Gard   58

5.
The Soil and the Sea   69
The Barbégal Watermill   81

6
New Cities… and How to Live   85
Vaison-la-Romaine: La Villasse and Puymin   95

7.
Bridges… and the Oldest Road in France   101
The Pont Julien   111

CONTENTS

8.
The Temples of their Gods 121
Nîmes: the Maison Carrée 125

9.
Theatres and Amphitheatres 135
Orange: the Theatre 140

10.
The Christian Takeover 153
Marseille: the Abbey Church of St.-Victor 164

Postscript: After the Romans 169

Further Reading 176

Selected Museums and Visitor Centres 178

Index 180

Author's Preface

The term 'Provence' can be misleading when applied to the area of southern France which the Romans ruled for 600 years. The word derives from the Latin *Provincia*, meaning 'the Province'. It was Julius Caesar who described this newly-conquered region as 'the Province of Rome'. And the name has stuck.

To make matters more complicated, Caesar's 'Province of Rome' was a great deal larger than the Provence of today, as the accompanying map shows. Almost two millennia of insurrections, invasions, religious conflict, feudal squabbles, dynastic greed and political shenanigans in general have shrunk the original *Provincia* to its present modest size.

In this book l have gone some way towards putting the clock back. I have concentrated on the area of present-day Provence and neighbouring Languedoc, which are the heartlands of the former Roman colony. But I have also extended my gaze further afield to take in sites which were once within the boundaries of the *Provincia*, and which still wear something of the glory that was Rome: in other words this book stretches westwards to include Roussillon and the foothills of the Pyrenees, eastwards to the Riviera and the Maritime Alps, and northwards along the Rhône Valley as far as Lyon.

On place-names, virtually all the sites mentioned in the text derive their present names from the Latin descriptions given them by the Romans—often themselves a rendering of Celtic or other local words which the Romans merely adapted. Where possible I have given both the Latin and the modern name (i.e. Massalia/Marseille), though for the sake of simplicity I have often used only the modern word. This may occasionally sound anachronistic, but seemed preferable to continual doubling-up.

My own response to the magnetism of Ancient Rome goes back to childhood. I remember paddling in a woodland stream in Sussex and suddenly coming across Roman tiles among the shingle, then taking

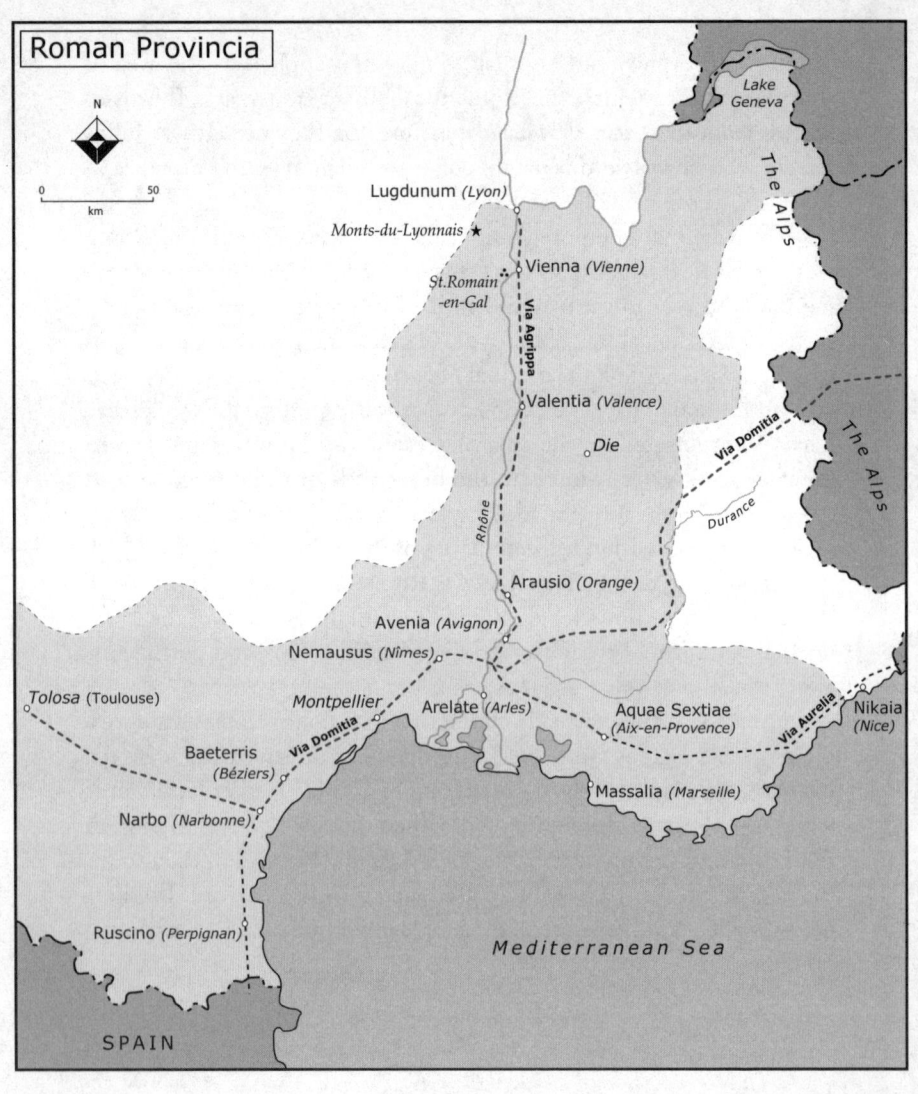

Preface

them excitedly to the local museum and being told that they must have come from a lost Roman villa that would have been close by. Later, as a teenager in Rome, I gazed in some awe at the vast hollow of the Pantheon, the labyrinthine Baths of Caracalla, and at the brutish majesty of the Coliseum.

Later still, as a roving journalist, I was astonished to come across entire Roman cities among the remote highlands of Algeria. But most vivid of all in my mind is of taking time off during a newspaper assignment in the Middle East to drive down into the desert of southern Syria to look at a Roman theatre which I knew to have remained virtually intact. A local guide led me round the place, and together we climbed to the very top of the stone terraces overlooking miles of scrub and scattered palm-groves. As we sat there in the sun I noticed that the stone bench between us was etched with shallow cups each about an inch across. I pointed these out to my guide, who responded with a nod and a grin. Still not saying anything he beckoned me to follow him. He led me out of the theatre and along the dusty back-streets of the town, and then gestured that we should go into a nearby café. It was a single room lit by a solitary electric light-bulb and furnished with bare wooden tables and a few rickety chairs. A group of men were seated at the far end of the room, smoking and drinking tea from tiny metal cups. My guide ordered us coffee, and as we made our way towards a nearby table he gave a grunt and grasped my elbow, then pointed to the group of men. I glanced across at them and saw that they were playing some kind of board game with dice and counters. And as I looked closer I noticed that the board was pitted with precisely the same pattern of shallow cups as on the stone bench high up on the terrace of the Roman theatre. My guide gave another grin, and we sipped our coffee.

So, Roman life goes on. Within the long stretch of the Roman Empire the Syrian desert is about as far as it is possible to travel from Provence, where I now live for part of each year. But the Romans cast their net wide, and under their rule certain ways of life became universal, and engrained. In Caesar's 'Province of Rome' it can often feel as if the Romans never really went away: they are still with us. They wove so much of the fabric of our lives. We owe to them so much, whether in matters of law, or for the roots of our language, or for just about everything to do with water: while here in Provence they have given us monuments and colossal engineering feats which dominate the landscape—bridges, aqueducts, amphitheatres, temples, baths, triumphal arches, and stretches of road that still bisect the countryside as if no one in the succeeding two thousand years has dared intrude on such perfect geometry.

This is the Provence of the Romans, as if it still belongs to them.

My chief debt of gratitude is to my wife Anne, who accompanied me on so many exploratory journeys across the region, putting together spectacular picnics which we ate under crumbling Roman aqueducts, and scrambling through vicious undergrowth to trace ancient paved roads and half-buried monuments. We both agreed that one of the benefits of undertaking this kind of research was to come across so many fascinating and hidden places that we would never otherwise have known to exist. I should like to add an extra word of thanks to our eager and tireless golden retriever, Star, who by now must have swum under more Roman bridges than any dog on record.

1.

THE EAGLE SPREADS ITS WINGS

It lasted six centuries—beginning more than a hundred years before the birth of Christ, and surviving long after the triumph of Christianity in Western Europe. Within that span of time the imprint of Rome upon the region we know as Provence was so massive that it remains indelible to this day. Caesar's 'Province of Rome' is with us wherever we care to look—in the towns and villages of the area, along its highways and rivers, and across its primordial landscape. Often larger than life, always astonishing, Roman Provence is a monument to an age of giants.

The epoch begins—as it will eventually end—in Marseille.

It was then a Greek city: Massalia (or Massilia). In about 600 BC a fleet of Greek merchants and adventurers from the west coast of Anatolia (today Turkey), along with their families and such possessions as they could take with them, fled the expanding Persian empire under Cyrus the Great and sailed westwards across the Mediterranean in search of a new home. Being sea-people they soon established a chain of coastal settlements in the region, the most important of which was the port of Massalia. It flourished. Massalia enjoyed a deep and spacious harbour well-hidden by protective cliffs, which made it ideal as a maritime trading-post. Furthermore, the long artery of the River Rhône offering access to the rich markets of Northern Europe, flowed into the sea only a short distance from the new city. Massalia rapidly became a key focus of commerce between east and west, north and south.

Then, with the emergence of the Roman republic as the dominant force in the Mediterranean, an alliance with the trading power of Massalia was a natural development. Political muscle and commercial know-how formed an ideal partnership. The alliance became particularly valuable to Rome once Carthage emerged as a serious threat to its su-

Coinage from the Greek city of Massalia (today Marseille), first century BC.

premacy in the region. It was a threat which came to a head with the legendary figure of Hannibal, the Carthaginian general who in 218 BC led his conquering army, elephants and all, up through Spain and over the Pyrenees, across southern Gaul and the Alps, and finally into Italy where he remained for sixteen long-years, posing a constant threat to Rome itself. Hannibal's passage through southern Gaul was facilitated by the cooperation of local tribes, whom he successfully bribed, and who no doubt were able to show him where elephants might successfully cross the mighty Rhône, and then to cross the even mightier Alps. These local tribes were no friends of the immigrant Greeks in their burgeoning young city. Hostility continued to mount, making the alliance with Rome even more advantageous to both sides. Rome would promise military protection, and in return the Greeks gave the Romans valuable trading privileges.

The Roman-Greek alliance was put to the test a mere twenty-one years after the final defeat of Hannibal in 202 BC. In 181 BC those local tribes mounted a serious threat to the city, and in response to an urgent appeal Rome sent an armed force which duly crushed the attackers. The Romans then departed. Twenty-seven years later a more serious threat met with the same response. And once again the soldiers were withdrawn. But aggression towards Massalia continued to escalate, aggravated by the growing prosperity and power of the Greek colony, which was now expanding in the shape of an outcrop of further settlements not only along the coast but far inland to include what are now

The Eagle Spreads its Wings

Avignon, Cavaillon and St. Rémy. The whole region was beginning to become a Greek colony.

It was in response to this expansionism that a number of hitherto separate local tribes were beginning to band together against the common enemy. And in 125 BC Rome answered an urgent appeal from Massalia for the third time. But now it was to be no brief military excursion. The Romans found themselves confronting not just a single opponent who could be dealt with, but a loose confederation of tribes who were spread over a wide area, and were a mixture of Ligurians—the occupants of the coastal region to the east—and a variety of semi-nomadic Celtic tribes of Germanic origin who had been drifting south in search of land. Over a period of two years the Roman army, infinitely better trained and equipped, took them on piecemeal, routing them one after the other.

The climax came in 123 BC. Led by their general, Caius Sextius Calvinus, the Romans inflicted a comprehensive defeat on the most dangerous of the Celtic tribes, the Salyens, taking their army into slavery and destroying their *oppidum*, or fortified capital, in the hills to the north of Massalia. After the victory the Roman general established a fortress where he could garrison his troops a short distance to the south, close to some warm springs. With typical Roman modesty he named the new settlement after himself, Aquae Sextiae, the Waters of Sextius, later abbreviated to Aix, and now Aix-en-Provence.

The Romans had come to stay. Ironically only a few insignificant fragments remain of Rome's first colonial settlement in Provence. Nothing could be less of a testimony to the grandeur that was Rome than Aix today. Even Sextius' famous waters no longer flow. On the other hand the Celtic capital he destroyed, the *oppidum* of Entremont, does survive, at least as a well-tended and well-guarded ruin on the northern outskirts of Aix, on a pine-scented hill amid carpets of wildflowers. The Celtic gods may have enjoyed a delayed revenge.

The leader of the defeated Salyens escaped both the slaughter and enslavement, and fled to another powerful and warlike Celtic tribe, the Allobroges, who controlled much of the Rhône valley to the west and north of the new Roman garrison. Flushed with victory over the Salyens the Romans arrogantly demanded that the chieftain be handed over. The demand was contemptuously ignored, whereupon Rome decided to intensify the conflict and within a year sent a far larger force into the troubled region, this time emulating the campaigns of Hannibal nearly a century earlier by including elephants among the fighting force. The target was now the Allobroges themselves, and the new military commander—soon to become the first Roman proconsul of the region—was a man who has the strongest claim to have been the founding father of Roman Provence. He was Domitius Ahenobarbus, soldier, aristocrat and—incidentally—grandfather of one of Julius Caesar's bitterest enemies.

Domitius not only crushed the Allobroges, but proceeded to annex all their lands, from the Rhône Valley to the Mediterranean and along the coast westwards as far as the Pyrenees. It was the beginning of Roman ownership of the entire region. And this was not just land-grabbing: there was a further motive on a grand scale. Since the defeat of Hannibal Rome already controlled the whole of Spain. All that separated Spain from Italy was southern Gaul. And the territory Domitius now annexed gave him the opportunity to create a land-link between the two. He began to build a road. In true Roman fashion it became a road that bears his name, the Via Domitia—one of the first great highways of the Roman Empire, about which a great deal more will be said in later chapters.

Like many of the major roads in history the Via Domitia had a key military function. For Rome to be the ruler of Spain was one thing: to control such a large subcontinent was quite another. There were constant uprisings in the peninsula, and so long as the only military access was by sea Rome was severely handicapped in trying to deal with them. The new road meant that armies could be based north of the Pyrenees, and, if needed, march into Spain within a few days. And so the great highway was begun. Domitius was in charge of operations, and set about surveying his newly-won lands with lofty dignity, taking a further leaf out of Hannibal's book by touring his conquered territories from the seat of an elephant.

Southern Gaul was now effectively a Roman colony, with Massalia a small Greek enclave many of whose numerous outposts had been taken over by Rome. But the new colony needed a capital. Aquae Sextiae was already an encampment: what was now required was an administrative centre. Domitius chose to create one on the very road he

The Eagle Spreads its Wings

was in the process of building. The choice was a former Celtic sea-port, open to the Mediterranean by way of a large and navigable lagoon. And in 118 BC it became the Roman settlement of Narbo (today Narbonne).

Before long the new capital was to give its name to the entire Roman province of southern Gaul: Gallia Narbonnensis. And the territory to be administered from Narbo included not only Provence and the Riviera as we know them today but extended westwards to Languedoc and Roussillon as far as the Pyrenees, and northwards to take in the entire Rhône Valley as far as Lyon, and what are now the French Alps as far as the shores of Lake Geneva. In fact, what is generally known simply as 'the Province' amounted to an enormous area.

Altogether, in less than a decade since answering Massalia's cry for help the Romans had truly arrived.

Yet, just as with Aix-en-Provence, almost nothing survives today of that first headquarters of Rome's first Gallic colony. Quite unlike Nîmes, a short distance away and founded not long afterwards, and which today positively overflows with Roman splendours, Narbonne

A fragment of the first Roman road in Gaul, the Via Domitia, preserved in Narbonne, then Narbo.

5

can boast little more than a fragment of Domitius' mighty highway, a few square yards of paving carefully preserved in its shallow pit in the central square of the city under the protective gaze of the Hôtel de Ville.

But it was a false dawn for the new colony. Even as Narbo was being established as the first Roman capital in Gaul, by the northern shores of Europe mass migrations of Germanic tribes were taking place, and those migrations were heading south. The two neighbouring tribes were the Cimbri and the Teutones, whose homeland was the low-lying area now known as Jutland, northern Denmark. It is believed that disastrous flooding from the sea may have driven the two tribes to seek fresh pastures. Whatever the reason they began to move southwards *en masse*, tens of thousands of them, men, women, children, livestock and all. Some historians have maintained that their only concern was to find new territories on which to settle, and that requests to local chieftains were repeatedly refused. Harsher voices have claimed that they were a murderous mob bent simply on plunder and mayhem. What is clear is that in the course of their slow drift southwards the two tribes were joined by others, so swelling the numbers of migrants on the move and offering an ever-increasing threat to any body of people bold enough to stand in their way.

By the year 109 BC they had crossed the Rhine and were now in territory controlled—nominally at least—by the new Roman colony. And now disaster struck. Alarmed by accounts of mass plunder and destruction, Rome dispatched successive armies against them. For all the professionalism they had displayed against rebellious mobs in the past, here were rapidly-recruited Roman soldiers led by generals appointed solely for political reasons, and they soon proved no match whatsoever for a force of battle-hardened warriors hungry for a promised land. By the year 105 BC three successive Roman armies had been routed and put to the sword. The final defeat is estimated to have cost 20,000 lives.

Rome was on the verge of panic. This was no disorganised barbarian rabble but a strongly-motivated fighting force that had proved itself more than a match for anything Rome could throw at it. What was more, the invaders were now on the very doorstep of the Roman heartland, posing a serious threat not only to the new colony in southern Gaul but to Italy and Rome itself. It was as if the ghost of Hannibal had returned. Drastic measures were needed.

The Eagle Spreads its Wings

Relief came in the shape of a man who has remained a folk-hero in Provence ever since. His name was Caius (or Gaius) Marius; and it has been claimed that one in four male children in Provence have born the name Marius, at least until recent times. He was not a member of Rome's ruling aristocracy: his fame and rise to power rested solely on his military prowess. At the time of the Germanic threat Marius was in command of an army fighting rebels in North Africa, and it was his success in this campaign that led to his recall to Rome, from where he was promptly sent to southern Gaul with the task of assembling and training an army to deal with the invading tribes.

From the outset fortune was on his side. For reasons that are obscure the two tribes split and went their separate ways. The Cimbri headed for northern Italy (where they were subsequently defeated) while the more powerful of the Germanic tribes, the Teutones, moved unopposed across Gaul into Spain, where they remained for more than two years to the discomfort of the local Iberian population. This digression provided Marius with invaluable time to build his army and to plan his campaign for the moment when the Teutones would resume their passage towards Rome, which was known to be their ultimate goal. And, like Hannibal more than a century earlier, in order to achieve this they would need to travel across the entire breadth of southern Gaul from west to east, from the Pyrenees to the Alps.

Marius was content to wait for them. And he used the time to make numerous preparations. First he put into practice a conviction that it was essential for success in modern warfare to maintain a standing army rather than a makeshift body of recruits assembled for a specific campaign and then dispersed, which had been the practice hitherto. The Roman historian Sallust, writing only half a century later, commented that Marius 'enrolled soldiers not according to their class... but allowing anyone to volunteer, for the most part the proletariat.' In doing so he created a modern-style army composed of career soldiers—except that the pay packet of the new Roman army tended to be loot and plunder, about which Sallust had nothing to say; and one cannot help wondering whether the farmers and stock-breeders of Roman Gaul relished the protection of Marius' new model army as much as did the administrators in their headquarters at Narbo. One of the drawbacks of recounting the historical events in Provence at this time is the absence of views from the local Gauls trying to lead their own lives amid these international cross-currents. Was it better to be pillaged by your protector, or by your enemy?

Marius put his new standing army to good use while they waited. At some stage the Teutones would need to cross the Rhône as they travelled towards Italy, and Marius decided to wait for them on the east bank of the river, close to the most likely crossing-point which was a ford near what is now the town of Beaucaire. The Rhône had treacherous currents and mud-flats, and as a supply-route from the sea it was far too unreliable. So he set his men to dig a canal from the naval base he created (now Fos) to his military camp close to what is today the city of Arles: in this way all the needs of his army could be transported directly from Italy, Marseille, or wherever.

While the canal was being constructed Marius waited. And he waited three years, receiving regular reports from Spain of the Teutones' movements, until the day when he knew precisely when and where they would be approaching, and in what numbers. He also learnt that another wandering tribe, the Ambrones, had joined the Teutones, so swelling the enemy numbers even more. The long-delayed engagement was about to begin.

The events that followed have come down to us as one of the epic dramas of the classical world. It was Homeric in scale, and appropriately so since the only written account of these events was from the pen of a Greek—a Greek, what is more, well-attuned to hearing the voices of the gods since he had been a priest at no less a shrine than the temple of Apollo at Delphi. His name was Plutarchos. Since his priesthood he had become Romanised as Plutarchus, and subsequently achieved universal fame as the first biographer of the Roman world. Plutarchus (to us simply Plutarch) wrote of the achievements of men who had contributed to the greatness of Greece and Rome. And one of these chosen heroes was Marius. Plutarch's *Life of Marius* includes an account of what was seen to be one of the decisive campaigns in the military history of Rome.

Just how accurate is Plutarch's account is naturally open to question since he wrote it more than a century after the death of Marius, and allowances almost certainly need to be made: soldiers' tales passed down over so many generations are bound to have acquired a certain unreal gloss. All the same, his story rings true, and vividly so: the smell and drama of events survived the long passage of time.

Picture the setting. The Roman army-in-waiting is encamped a short distance to the west of the Rhône, roughly halfway between what today are the cities of Avignon and Arles, and close to where the Teutones will need to cross the river. There seems to have been no viable alternative (and it was probably where Hannibal had made his crossing with elephants a century earlier). To the south the Rhône splits into numerous ever-changing rivulets amid a wilderness of salt-marsh and floodwater (today the Camargue). An army could drown here. To the north it is no easier: the current flows more swiftly between high rocks. But between the two, the water is shallower and there is a ford of sorts, adequate for people to make the crossing along with their animals, livestock, carts and possessions. Accordingly this is the strategic place for Marius to guard. He also has his own defensive position, which he will soon use: this is a range of serrated hills called the Alpilles (the small Alps) which rise a short distance to the rear of his encampment. The Alpilles form a dramatic labyrinth of bleached and jagged rocks into which he can easily withdraw. From here ten thousand eyes can safely watch an invading force as it passes across the open plain below.

And this is precisely what did happen.

The Teutones steadily made their way eastwards towards the Rhône, drawing ever closer to the waiting Roman army, finally making the crossing where Marius had anticipated. 'Soon they came in sight,' wrote Plutarch, 'in numbers beyond belief.' He estimated their number to be as many as 300,000. This was certainly an exaggeration—how would he have known? Even so, this was no ordinary army on the march: here was a huge migrant population, animals and personal belongings included. And they had been accustomed to travelling in this fashion for more than a decade. It must have looked like a human tide. As for the armed soldiers among them, Plutarch reported that they were 'of a terrible aspect, uttering strange cries and shouts'.

Marius by this time seems to have withdrawn his troops to the shelter of the Alpilles, from where he could observe and assess the enemy as they massed on the plain to the south, taking great care not to engage them until a time came when he would be ready to do so. Plutarch describes the scene as the two armies faced one another for the first time.

ROMAN PROVENCE

A nineteenth-century impression of an entire tribe of Teutones on the move south into Roman Provence, wives, children and livestock included.

'Taking up a great part of the plain with their camp, they challenged Marius to battle. He seemed to take no notice of them, but kept his soldiers within their fortifications... He placed the soldiers by turns upon the bulwarks, to survey the enemy, and so made them familiar with their appearance and voices, which were indeed altogether extravagant and barbarous, and he caused them to observe their arms, and their way of using them, so that in a little time what at first appeared terrible to their apprehension, by frequent viewing became familiar.'

In adopting this effective psychological approach Marius was guided by an unexpected member of his high command. According to Plutarch she was a Syrian woman by the name of Martha, and she was a prophetess. So highly esteemed was she that Marius had her 'solemnly carried about in a litter'. He would even 'perform sacrifices by her direction... and when she went to sacrifice she wore a purple robe lined and buckled up, and had in her hand a little spear trimmed with ribbons and garlands.' The purple robe is an indication of the esteem in which Marius held her. Purple, or Tyrian purple as it became known, was the rarest of all dyes, obtained only from murex shells found on a single island off the Phoenician coast near Tyre. Its rarity value made it generally the preserve of kings and chieftains. (The Catholic Church later adopted this exclusive practice when adorning its own bishops, and continues to do so.)

Marius' purpose in refusing to join battle with the Teutones was to encourage them to continue on their way eastwards so that he could then trail them before selecting his place to attack. Plutarch describes how the Teutones in frustration finally packed up their baggage and began to 'move past the Roman camp, where the greatness of their number was especially made evident by the long time they took in their march, for they were said to be six days continually going past Marius' fortifications.'

They had played into Marius' hands. And he followed them, shadowing them at a safe distance, pitching camp after camp as the two armies moved slowly eastwards. Plutarch reports that from this point onwards two vultures appeared, flying high above Marius' soldiers as they marched. Plutarch, as a Greek priest of Delphi and a historian, would have been familiar with the legend that the presence of vultures accompanying an army was a prophecy of victory, and that the Persian emperor Cyrus the Great had even equipped his soldiers with tunics bearing the image of a vulture. And so, according to Plutarch, the progress of Marius' army was tracked by two vultures constantly in attendance as it stealthily shadowed the vast throng of the Germanic tribes moving eastwards. Their route traversed the southern fringes of the Alpilles, then crossed the open plain south of the first Roman settlement of Aquae Sextiae founded eighteen years earlier, until they reached a broad low-lying region of rivers and moist fields that was curtained by formidable mountain ranges on three sides, to the north, east and south. This was the terrain Marius chose as the place finally to engage the enemy.

It was here, before the encircling backdrop of those towering mountains, that the historic battle took place—one that set the seal on the Roman conquest of southern Gaul. With Marius' forces deployed cunningly in different places the invaders were outwitted and outflanked, caught in a pincer movement, and finally lured into attacking the main Roman army uphill. The outcome was a rout. 'The Romans,' in Plutarch's words, 'pursued them, slew and took prisoners above one hundred thousand,' until the little River Arc in the valley below was stained with blood. With a touch of black humour he added: 'They say that the inhabitants... made fences round their vineyards with the bones, and that the ground, enriched by the moisture of the putrefied bodies, next season yielded a prodigious crop.'

Today the River Arc is a gentle stream meandering through water-meadows. On higher ground a little to the north stands the village of Pourrières. It is claimed by some historians that the name derives from the Latin *putridus*, referring of course to those 'putrefied bodies' described by Plutarch. (Plutarch wrote in Greek, not Latin, and the Greek word for 'putrid', or 'rotten', is—in Roman letters—'PUON', which sounds somewhat further away. So, the connection has to remain uncertain.) What is undeniable is that the present village is certainly the site of the final strategic camp from which Marius launched his triumphant attack, a fact proudly acknowledged today in Gallic fashion in the form of a street named after him, Rue Caius Marius, as well as—more bizarrely—a small nineteenth-century pyramid raised in his honour over the local fountain.

More evocative than any memorial is the outlook from a commanding position high up on the edge of Pourrières, overlooking the long slope southwards. It was here that the soldiers of the Teutones tried to attack the Roman army, only to be driven back and slaughtered in the plain below along the banks of the River Arc.

But the most eloquent witness of all is the pale flank of a mountain to the west which presides over this former battlefield like a long white wave about to break upon the plain. After Marius' final triumph the mountain became known as the Montagne de la Victoire, as though its very presence had given a blessing to the Roman army. Many centuries later it itself became canonised (unofficially at least) as if in Christian thanksgiving for having delivered Provence from the hands of the barbarian hordes. And so it became Mont (or Montagne) Ste.-Victoire. In more recent times it has also become 'Cézanne's mountain', the peak he loved and gazed at daily from his studio outside Aix, and which he painted in so many moods and seasons.

Yet Mont Ste.-Victoire will always remain the noblest shrine to Marius, and a monument to the defining moment when this region of southern Gaul became unquestionably a possession of Rome, and remained so for the next six hundred years.

The Eagle Spreads its Wings

Apart from the sacred mountain and a wealth of stirring legends nothing survives of that heroic moment in the early history of Roman Provence. But then the true legacy of Marius is invisible: it lies in the fact that without his historic victory over the Germanic tribes there might never have been a Roman Provence at all; and all the striking monuments and feats of engineering which we now applaud would never have existed.

Les Baux-de-Provence: *Les Tremaïe*

There is one intriguing candidate for a lasting memorial to Marius and his hour of glory. At the heart of that spectacular range of jagged hills to the west of Aix known as the Alpilles, from where Marius had gazed down at the barbarian tribes as they passed by for six whole days, rises the mediaeval citadel and ruined castle of Les Baux, high on its dramatic plateau. On a south-facing slope below the castle is a triangular block of limestone some twenty-five feet in height, relatively inconspicuous in a rough terrain of scrub and boulders. On the face of the rock is a carving in low-relief of three standing figures, a little under life-size. They are of a man and two women, apparently in Roman clothing, and experts have generally agreed that the carvings date from the Augustan period about the time of the birth of Christ.

Not generally agreed is their identity. Broadly speaking there are three schools of thought: the romantic, the orthodox Christian, and the prosaic. The romantic interpretation is that the three figures represent Marius—one of the few known portraits of the great general—his wife Julia and Martha, the Syrian prophetess. Support for this argument, in addition to the plausible date, lies in the fact that the male figure is dressed in the simple toga of a Roman consul, which Marius was. In addition the supposed figure of Martha is wearing what could well be an oriental headdress appropriate for her Middle Eastern origin. It remains unclear why such a commemorative plaque should have been placed here some hundred years later, unless it was that in the high noon of Roman power it was deemed appropriate to honour the saviour of Provence by showing him forever gazing out over the land he had saved.

ROMAN PROVENCE

Ruins of the theatrically-placed mediaeval hill-town and château of Les Baux-de-Provence, built on the site of an important Roman and pre-Roman settlement.

If the romantic interpretation is a little thin on evidence, then the Christian version is scarcely more than pious fantasy—except in one important respect: it offers a surprising link to one of the most touching early Christian legends, which caught the imagination of much of Europe towards the end of the Roman era and in the centuries to follow. This is the legend of the Three Marys, all of them followers of Christ, who were said to have drifted to these shores on a raft shortly after the Crucifixion—about which there will be more in a later chapter. At some time early in the Christian era the three figures in the Les Baux carving were believed to represent Mary Magdalene, her sister Martha and her brother Lazarus, all of them survivors of the raft. Very possibly it was the name Martha, common to both interpretations, which supplied the link between the two legends, Martha the Syrian prophetess becoming Martha the sister of Mary Magdalene, and her supposedly eastern headdress becoming interpreted as a mitre. Less easy to comprehend is the name awarded to the carving, *Les Tremaïe*, the Three Marys, since one of

On the hillside below Les Baux the mysterious Roman rock-carving of three figures known as *Les Tremaïe*, the subject of many intriguing interpretations.

the figures is unmistakably male. Yet such is the name still given to it in guidebooks, as it is to the tiny nineteenth-century chapel erected immediately below the carved rock.

Amid so many confusions and conjectures the rational choice would seem to be the third interpretation—the prosaic one, which is to admit that no one has ever come up with a convincing explanation for this mysterious carving on its lonely hillside, and that it may simply be the funerary memorial to some Roman family whose identity is forever lost. And yet it appears so much more important than a mere tombstone: what we see is a huge triangular slab of rock that has been skillfully carved high above ground level with three distinctive figures apparently looking across the plain towards the distant coast. Here the imagination begins to take wing, and the romantic interpretation grows more plausible. The figure on the left becomes Marius; and between him and his wife stands his mentor, the prophetess Martha. It was she who had advised him to let the barbarian hordes pass by unhindered, however provoked his soldiers might be to launch an attack. Perhaps, then, it is this crucial moment in the campaign that the three figures are witnessing from their eyrie: the passage of hostile tribes crossing the plain below over a period of six days, with Marius following the advice of the prophetess: let them pass, let them pass.

Whether such an interpretation of the *Tremaïe* is valid or not, the theatrical setting of the Alpilles feels appropriate for Marius. It is his territory. To the west was the canal he dug across the stony wilderness of the Crau to bring supplies for his troops from the coast. To the east lies the plain where he finally trapped the invading army, as well as the presiding mountain which still honours his triumph, Mont Ste.-Victoire. And a short distance to the north, wedged into the slopes of the Alpilles, is a place he would have known intimately, and which he would very likely have used as a safe haven when the Germanic tribes were approaching. This was Glanum, a short distance to the south of St.-Rémy de Provence—a town lost almost without trace for centuries, then rediscovered and excavated in the 1920s.

No ancient site in Provence is more dramatic than Glanum. The bristling peaks of the Alpilles rising on three sides make it one of the most evocative archaeological sites in the western world. What we see

The Eagle Spreads its Wings

The Celtic/Greek/Roman city of Glanum, dramatically set in a cleft of the Alpilles close to St.-Rémy.

today is to some extent the remains of a Roman settlement dating from shortly after Marius' time. Yet much of the place is a shell of the town he would have known, with its Sacred Way winding into a cleft of the hills to a hidden spring revered for its healing powers. No doubt the scent of pines and the chorus of cicadas which today fill the summer air would have been familiar to him too. Originally Glanum was an Iron Age settlement dating from as early as the seventh century BC. Then, over the following centuries it grew into an important *oppidum*, inhabited predominantly by Celts, who named the place after one of their gods, Glan. And at the heart of the settlement, bringing fame and growing prosperity to the place, was that sacred spring with its curative waters.

The Celtic people who occupied and developed Glanum were the Salyens, the very tribe whose headquarters at Entremont (near Aix) was destroyed by the Romans some twenty years before Marius' campaign. By this time the Celtic population of Glanum was becoming overshadowed by Greeks moving here from Massalia a short distance to the south. The Greeks further expanded and enriched the town. And much of what they added—a marketplace, town hall, residential buildings, shops, temples—survives today at least in embryo, contributing to what is held to be the finest example of Gallo-Greek culture in France.

This is the Glanum Marius would have known during those three years of waiting for the Germanic tribes to approach. After his victory over them he departed for Rome, and never returned. Yet a thread of family history was to link him to the future of Roman Provence and of the Roman Empire in general. In 100 BC, two years after Marius' victory over the Teutones at Pourrières, his wife Julia, who came from a distinguished Roman family, became an aunt to a newborn boy. Thirty years later the boy, by now a rising power in the land, gave the funeral oration in Rome for his aunt who had been the widow of a legendary general he deeply admired. Soon his own celebrity would match that of Marius himself, not least in this region of southern Gaul.

Julia's young nephew was Julius Caesar.

2.
CAESAR AND CAESAR

Less than half a century separates the victory of Marius over the Germanic tribes and the arrival in 58 BC of Julius Caesar as the governor who would soon name the new colony 'the Province of Rome'.

Caesar's ambitions far outstretched the mere controlling and administering of his Province. Such matters he left to able minions, at least while more pressing business was on hand. Caesar was a soldier, warlord and empire-builder, and from the outset the colony he now governed served principally as a platform from which he could pursue the most demanding campaign Rome had so far undertaken, namely the conquest of the whole of Gaul.

This southern stretch of Gaul had already been in Roman hands for half a century. Now Caesar wanted all the rest of it. The military operation in pursuit of this vast ambition, which was to make his name and his fortune, occupied him for the next seven years. And during this time the Province served as his base-camp, a recruiting centre for his army, a vital supply-route via the port of Massalia and even as his troops' food-store.

The intervening five decades since the departure of Marius had seen further tremors of rebellion from the local tribes. Twelve years after Marius' victory at Pourrières came the final uprising of the once-powerful Salyens, whose headquarters at Entremont had long ago been destroyed, and whose city and holy shrine of Glanum had already been taken over first by Greek settlers from Massalia and subsequently by the Romans themselves. The ultimate defeat of the Salyens in 98 BC is the last we hear of them as a coherent body. Presumably they blended into the landscape, so to speak, becoming part of the indigenous population of the region resigned to the authority of Rome, paying her taxes and being recruited for service in the conqueror's army. Then, four years before Caesar's arrival another indigenous tribe, the Allobroges, who were based in the Rhône Valley with their capital at what is now Vienne, mounted a revolt, and were duly suppressed by the Roman legions, just as they had been by Domitius nearly three-quarters of a century before.

(It is a measure of the Romans' dominance that this was to be the last serious threat to their rule in the Province until the final crushing invasion by the Visigoths more than five hundred years later, which brought it all to an end.)

The fate of conquered tribes was an uncertain one. Local rebellions such as those of the Salyens and the Allobroges might result in the loss of their leaders in captivity, whereas the common footsoldier/peasant was likely to return to his former life, perhaps now with a Roman landowner to command his services. But with migrant, or invading, tribes the price of defeat was more often slavery, for men and women alike. This had been the fate of the Germanic tribes defeated by Marius at Pourrières, when more than one hundred thousand were taken prisoner, according to Plutarch. Rome thrived on being a slave society, sometimes with brutally dramatic results. In 71 BC, the year before the young Julius Caesar delivered the funeral oration in Rome for his aunt, the widow of Marius, the city had celebrated the final defeat of Spartacus, the legendary slave who took on the might of the Roman state, and for a while shook it to its roots. In the immediate aftermath of his defeat the citizens of Rome, and very possibly Caesar himself since he was certainly there, were entertained by the spectacle of six thousand of Spartacus' fellow-slaves crucified along the length of the Appian Way.

Provence did not inherit a gentle conqueror.

※

'All Gaul is divided into three parts': so runs the celebrated opening of Caesar's *Gallic Wars*. He left out the fourth part—the Province (today Provence, Languedoc, Roussillon and the Rhône Valley)—since this region had already been part of the Roman Empire for almost three-quarters of a century. Throughout the seven years of the Gallic wars the Province seems to have given unwavering support to Caesar in his campaigns: not that the local inhabitants are likely to have been given much choice in the matter. Military service was compulsory, and it is recorded that soldiers recruited from the Province formed an invaluable limb of Caesar's army, particularly as cavalry. Celtic tribesmen, many of them long resistant to Roman rule, now found themselves fighting alongside their conquerors, bearing arms against fellow-Celts who may formerly have been their comrades in arms. Such was the weight of Roman colonial power.

That said, it is something of an anachronism to describe loyalties in such terms. It is estimated that Gaul as a whole was populated at this time by between two and three hundred different tribes, mostly of Celtic origin, who had drifted westwards from east of the River Rhine two or three centuries earlier in search of fresh pastures. They were for the most part farmers and cattle-breeders, many of them still semi-nomadic, or else living in scattered communities round a fortified *oppidum* where the tribal chieftain 'held court'. They were in no sense a nation. Caesar himself dismissed them as 'trousered and moustached barbarians' who were forever divided among themselves into warring factions—which made it all the easier for him to subdue them, one by one.

The one occasion when a coherent opposition was mounted was under the inspired leadership of Vercingetorix, one of the Celtic chieftains, whose army came perilously close to driving Caesar's legions out of Gaul, until he was outmanoeuvred and finally crushed in 52 BC, and for his pains spent the next six years in captivity before being paraded

A nineteenth-century vision of the legendary Gallic chieftain, Vercingetorix, who successfully united local tribes against Julius Caesar's army until finally defeated in 52 BC.

in Rome as a trophy and then strangled. It was an unheroic end for one of France's favourite heroes. (His comic-strip reincarnation, Asterix, has fared a good deal better.) For his campaign against Vercingetorix Caesar received invaluable support from one of the local tribes, the Allobroges. They had formerly rebelled against Roman rule (and been crushed in 68 BC); but now they opened their capital in the Rhône Valley to Caesar. This was Vienne, soon to become a Roman colony and one of the wealthiest cities in all Roman Gaul. Today the boundaries of Caesar's Province have shrunk, and Vienne is no longer within the borders of modern Provence: none the less historically it deserves to be included, and the city preserves handsome monuments of its Roman past. This may be a good moment to slip in the fact that among the more curious of these monuments is an ungainly pyramid known as the Plan de l'Aiguille ('needle'), which has given rise to numerous legends as to its original purpose and function, the most far-fetched being that it was specially erected by Pontius Pilate to be his tomb.

Caesar's own account of the Gallic wars remains the foremost historical account of the campaign. What it lacks, naturally enough, is an objective view of the man himself, and his motives for undertaking so colossal an enterprise. It is here that a later Roman historian provides some sharp insights, freed by the passage of time from any need for sycophancy. He was Gaius Suetonius, actually a Greek (like his forerunner Plutarch), and his major surviving work, written about the year 121 AD, is a series of biographical sketches beginning with Julius Caesar and continuing with the eleven Roman emperors who followed him. The book is known as *The Twelve Caesars*, and it is a goldmine of factual reporting, mixed with hearsay and salacious gossip, all of it offered with a blunt and refreshing honesty: 'Caesar surveyed the many provinces open to him and chose Gaul as being the likeliest to supply him with wealth and triumph... His nine years of governorship produced the following result. He reduced to the form of a province the whole of Gaul enclosed by the Pyrenees, the Alps, the Cevennes, the Rhine and the Rhône—about 640,000 square miles in all... And he extracted an annual tribute of 400,000 gold pieces.'

Suetonius goes on to claim that 'in Gaul he plundered large and small temples'; while a further aspect of Caesar's insatiable greed was his appetite for 'affairs with women, commonly described as numerous and time the third contestant in the Roman power struggle, Crassus, was dead, leaving Pompey and Caesar to fight it out between them. Both Massalia and Arelate were independent states: Massalia had always been so, while Arelate was yet to be formally embraced as a Roman colony. With Pompey's fleet sailing close by, and Caesar and his army on shore, suddenly the theatre of war was shifting to Provence for what was to be the final act of the civil war.

The fact that Massalia was a port whose wealth and livelihood depended on the sea may have influenced its rulers to favour Pompey, whose fleet was nearby and needed an anchorage. Accordingly seven of Pompey's galleys were berthed in the great harbour under the command of his lieutenant, Domitius Ahenobarbus, a name that would have garnered recognition and respect as belonging earlier to the man who had been the first Roman proconsul in the region and responsible for beginning the ambitious highway westwards towards Spain, the Via Domitia (see Chapter 1). Now the grandson had become one of Julius Caesar's bitterest enemies.

The decision by Arelate to support Caesar rather than Pompey proved to be the making of that city: it is why to this day Arles offers proof of having been at one time the most important Roman city beyond the borders of Italy. Caesar's response to that offer of support was to order twelve galleys to be built there in order to confront Pompey's fleet. It was a commission which, allowing for the exaggeration of hindsight, is reputed to have been carried out within thirty days. What made the enterprise feasible at all was the canal linking Arelate directly to the port of Fos, which Marius had constructed more than half a century earlier. While Caesar's army was laying siege to Massalia from the land the new galleys made their way down Marius' canal and along the coast to join the siege from the sea.

Caesar handed command of the vessels to a man who, according to the historian Plutarch, was 'so trusted by Caesar that he was entered in his will as his second heir'. He was Decimus Brutus. (Just four years later, on the Ides of March 44 BC, Brutus was to be the third assassin to plunge his dagger into Caesar. 'You too, my child?' are reputed to have been Caesar's dying words, a touching reference to his paternal feelings absent in Shakespeare's more familiar version, *Et tu, Brute?*) After a six-month siege Massalia capitulated. A vengeful Caesar proceeded to

extravagant. These included several senators' wives, and several que
the most famous of these being Cleopatra of Egypt,' who bore hi
son. Suetonius even quotes a popular Gallic song of the times refer
to him as 'our bald whoremonger'. Hardly the portrait of Julius Ca
painted in school history-books.

Once the Gallic wars were over the Provençal city which beca
most closely associated with Julius Caesar was Arles. From the vi
point of the Roman conquerors nowhere in the Province was m
strategically placed. Its position near the mouth of the Rhône mad
an ideal commercial crossroads between the Mediterranean cities a
those of central and northern Europe. The Rhône was an artery an
lifeline, and Arles became an *entrepôt* for trade from both north a
south. It was equally important militarily, being located at a convenie
halfway station between Italy and Spain. Before the Roman takeo
the city seems to have been a largely Greek trading post: a spur of t
flourishing Greek port of Massalia. The town had been set up on a roc
outcrop at the northern tip of the Rhône delta overlooking the marsl
wilderness of the Camargue, and was known by the Greek inhabitan
as Theline. Then, with the arrival of Caesar it acquired a new name, an
an appropriate one: Arelate, meaning 'the town in the marshes'.

Largely by accident Arelate/Arles came to play a key role in Roma
domestic politics. In Rome the republic was in the throes of a prolonge
power struggle between three rival generals. The three warlords were
Crassus (the general who had finally destroyed Spartacus), Pompey ('the
Great' as he became known) and Julius Caesar. In 49 BC rivalry erupted
into civil war when Caesar 'crossed the Rubicon', so giving posterity its
most familiar epithet for describing an irreversible action. Caesar's
action was to lead an army south into Roman Italy across what was only
a small river, but which marked the boundary between the conquered
provinces to the north and the republic itself. In doing so Caesar was violating a law of the Roman senate forbidding any such action unless
soldiers were first disarmed. Caesar's gesture was seen—rightly—as a
declaration of war. 'The die is cast,' Caesar is reputed to have declared.

The convolutions of the civil war in Italy lie beyond the boundaries
of *Roman Provence*, except for one strategic event which took place in
that same year, 49 BC, when the two Provençal cities of Arelate and
Massalia found themselves on opposite sides of the conflict. By this

strip the Greek city of its treasures, its trading privileges and most of its territories, the chief beneficiary being Arelate, which expanded in wealth and prosperity from that moment onwards. In Massalia the outcome was bittersweet. With defeat imminent Pompey is reported to have galloped away from the city in disguise, making his way to Egypt where he was unceremoniously murdered by the courtiers of King Ptolemy. Caesar, arriving in Egypt in October 48 BC, was presented with his former rival's head, and refused even to look at it.

Within a few years of Caesar's victory over Pompey the newly-enriched city of Arelate became officially designated a Roman colony. It became Caesar's 'little Rome in Gaul' and it blossomed commercially. Yet at the same time there was a price to be paid for being embraced by Rome. Now that the wars were over—first the long campaign in Gaul and then the civil war—there were Roman legions to be disbanded and hence a great many soldiers to be resettled. The question was: where? In a Roman army there was no system of pensions. Soldiers were supposed to look after themselves. But in such large numbers this could be disruptive to the state. Instead Caesar came up with an alternative: the gift of land. Within the republic itself such a solution would have involved dispossessing Roman citizens, and would therefore have been unacceptable. But in conquered territories no such legal rights interfered, and Caesar took full advantage. Eviction orders handed out to local farmers and landowners were a blunt reminder that, for all the supposed benefits of stability and the *Pax Romana*, the inhabitants of the Province were living under the yoke of foreign military rule. In the general handout instituted by Caesar, Arelate, including the Camargue and other surrounding areas, was given to soldiers of the Roman 6th Legion. Later other veterans benefited in the same way, among them soldiers who had taken part in the invasion of Britain. Arelate became to a large extent a settlement for foreign immigrants.

As for the other three new colonies established in the Province during the aftermath of the civil war, each became similarly 'colonised'. Veterans of the Roman 10th Legion were settled at Narbo (Narbonne). The 7th Legion was given what is now Béziers, and the 8th Legion awarded Fréjus (a settlement established by Caesar on the new road being planned to lead to Italy, the Via Aurelia, and duly named after him, Forum Julii).

To soften the widespread resentment created by so many evictions Caesar took the precaution of buttressing the power of local leaders, buying their support with gifts and tax concessions, even the ultimate prize of Roman citizenship. Doubtless, too, for the population as a whole there would have been economic benefits of living within a dynamic and well-organised state, sufficient at least to blunt any spirit of rebellion.

In all, within the span of a few years the impact of Caesar on the 'Province of Rome' had been felt everywhere. It was the beginning of a process in which the native people of Gaul were to find their lives gradually but irreversibly altered—in matters of law, social habits, loyalties, religion and ultimately even day-to-day language. To a large extent Caesar's *Pax Romana* put an end to traditional tribal conflicts, providing a new sense of security—provided, of course, that the Gallic people accepted the yoke of Roman authority. And for those relatively few whose skills or good fortune led them to become drawn into Roman life the door was open to countless privileges: they were able to join the ranks of officialdom, even to attain high office, to enjoy the hedonistic pleasures of Roman life (the baths, the theatres and amphitheatres) and to acquire that ultimate passport to worldly success, Roman citizenship. The successful Gaul might come to feel his true fatherland was Italy, just as his language, both at home and at work, was now Latin and not the Celtic tongue of his forebears. Furthermore it was a language that could be written, and which he had learnt to write.

But all this was to come later, with Caesar's successors. Meanwhile, within a brief span of time, Caesar himself was dead, assassinated in Rome. Suetonius' account of the murder, and of the omens and prophecies leading up to it, is vivid and succinct (incidentally providing Shakespeare with much material for *Julius Caesar*). It was far from being the only murder recounted in Suetonius' biography of *The Twelve Caesars*. Of those twelve rulers seven were assassinated, two committed suicide and only three died of natural causes Events in Rome itself offer a chilling contrast to the relative peace enjoyed by Roman Provence over those centuries. The *Pax Romana* seems to have worked better abroad than at home.

There is one surprising footnote to the story of Julius Caesar's relationship with Provence, and Arles in particular. In the autumn of the

The real Julius Caesar. The only known portrait-bust of him done during his lifetime, found in the River Rhône at Arles in 2008.

year 2008 archaeologists conducted an underwater exploration of the Rhône riverbed close to the city. A substantial cache of Roman artefacts was brought to the surface, the most remarkable find being a stone bust of a man, startlingly lifelike and in almost pristine condition. To the archaeologist in charge the face was instantly familiar: it matched precisely the features on coins minted in Rome around the year 50 BC. In fact the bust was nothing less than a portrait of Julius Caesar. What was more, it was the only known portrait head of Caesar made during his lifetime.

Unlike the later convention of representing Roman rulers as divine beings (and about as personal as a tailor's dummy), this head is strikingly realistic—the stern mouth, wrinkled skin, balding head. It can only have been done from life. Caesar may have actually sat for the artist. The generally accepted view is that the bust was carved soon after Caesar's triumph over Pompey in Massalia at a time when he was showering privileges on Arelate, and that out of gratitude it would have occupied a prominent place in some public building in the city. But then, why should it have ended up in the Rhône? What seems likely is that after Caesar's murder by Brutus a few years later the city fathers took the pragmatic and somewhat ignoble decision not to risk offending his assassins, and so dumped the bust of their former patron in the river. So much for the glorious conqueror of Gaul.

One of Suetonius' twelve Caesars—and in terms of political success certainly the greatest of them—was the grand-nephew of Julius Caesar, in whose will he was adopted as Julius' son and heir. This was Octavius, who as Augustus Caesar was to become the first Roman to assume the title of emperor. In Provence the legacy of Augustus is even more dominant than that of Julius Caesar—in the theatres and amphitheatres of the region, its temples and aqueducts, roads and bridges, fortifications and thermal baths, not to mention those outsize statues of the mighty ruler who straddled the Roman world for forty-four years and came to be treated as a god. Those extraordinary achievements, many of them only completed long after his death, are the subject of the main body of this book. But first the man himself.

Historians have labelled Augustus as one of the great administrative geniuses of history, largely on the grounds that he single-handedly re-organised virtually every aspect of Roman life both in Italy and in the expanded empire, including of course the Province. For his entire reign it was ruled by a governor who was personally appointed by the emperor and answerable directly to him. The long shadow of Augustus was cast over the region, whether he was present or not. Then there are more sceptical voices which have described him as a political gangster and warlord who, having got his way by brute force, then strove to be seen as a legitimate head of state (though what would have constituted a legitimate head of state in these bellicose times is hard to imagine). What is impossible to dispute is that without him the Roman Empire might not have survived even into the first century AD, and certainly not for a further four-and-a-half centuries—in which case there would have been no Roman Provence worth speaking of, and the region would have been deprived of much of its present character and magic.

Suetonius describes a prophecy circulating in Rome in 63 BC that a king would soon be born who would rescue the ailing republic. This was the year of Augustus' birth. Suetonius offers a protracted account of how Augustus (or Octavius as he still was) systematically eliminated his rival generals bidding to succeed Julius Caesar, culminating in the final victory over Mark Antony and Cleopatra in the battle of Actium, after which the Roman Senate awarded him the title 'Augustus', meaning 'the Revered One'. He was now the ruler of the entire Roman world, and as supreme ruler he saw to it that he would indeed be revered.

Suetonius then devotes a great deal of space to describing the unexpected modesty of his way of life, with his ordinary Roman house and ordinary Roman meals. He adds, with a wry smile, that it was said of Augustus how he would sometimes commit adultery, but only for reasons of state, never out of passion. Suetonius also comments that Augustus liked to invite his dinner guests to adopt the persona of one of the gods, and that he himself would choose to be Apollo, the sun-god. As for his appearance, 'He was unusually handsome and exceedingly graceful at all periods of his life,' Suetonius explains. 'He had clear, bright eyes, in which he liked to have it thought that there rested a kind of divine power; and it greatly pleased him, whenever he looked keenly at anyone, if that person let his face fall as if before the radiance of the sun.'

Certainly Augustus as the sun-god would have been a familiar image to anyone living in the towns and cities of Roman Provence at this time. Like all dictators ever since he made sure that his statues, like his authority, were everywhere, and extremely large.

Augustus paid two extended visits during his forty-four years as Caesar, the first of them in the very year he was proclaimed 'the Revered One': 27 BC. One of his decisions on arrival was to give prominence to the town of Narbo by establishing it as the administrative capital of the entire Roman colony of southern Gaul soon to be known as Gallia Narbonnensis or, simply, 'the Province'. Narbo, as we have seen, had been founded (or taken over from the Celts) in the very early days of Roman occupation by Domitius as a key staging post and port on the planned new road to Spain. Since then its population had been greatly swollen by Julius Caesar's decision to settle veterans of the Roman 10th Legion in the town. But now it enjoyed the status of a colonial capital.

In addition to Narbo/Narbonne, one other town in the region owes much to that first visit to the Province of Augustus Caesar, and that is Fréjus. Today it is a coastal town and holiday resort on the Côte d'Azur, but at that time it was known by the title given it by Julius Caesar, Forum Julii. Besides being an important staging-post on the new coastal road to Italy Fréjus was also a port. And it was here that Augustus brought one of the greatest trophies of his long career, the defeated fleet of Mark Antony.

Of all Augustus' rivals for supreme power Mark Antony was the last and the most formidable. His final downfall, along with that of Cleopatra, at the battle of Actium in 31 BC has been minutely and painfully documented (as well as dramatised by Shakespeare), along with their ritual suicide which followed. The final sea-battle at Actium was in the end an ignominious one, and much has been made of Cleopatra's sudden departure and Antony's pursuit of her. Two Roman historians have left accounts of Antony's fleet. Plutarch claims that it consisted of at least 300 vessels, while Tacitus tells us of its fate after the battle—how elements of that fleet were brought by Augustus from the eastern Mediterranean all the way here to the coast of the Province at Forum Julii.

Augustus did not arrive in the Province until the year he became emperor (and acquired his new name), already four years after the battle of Actium, by which time Antony's captive fleet may already have been moored here. The harbour at Forum Julii had been formed from a natural lagoon linked to the open sea by a canal. There are records that it still existed as a harbour in the Middle Ages, but since then the gradual recession of the sea has entirely obliterated it. Where Antony's vessels were once moored are now fields patrolled by bright-coloured butterflies and flanked by a rash of scattered modern buildings. Those with sharp eyes and a keen sense of geography can still make out something of the harbour's original outline in the shape of raised dykes and the general lay-out of the land: otherwise only one piece of actual evidence survives. This is a battered-looking hexagonal tower standing amid the scrub and known optimistically as the Lanterne d'Auguste. Whether or not a light of some description was once placed within it, and whether or not Augustus personally ordered its construction, the function of the tower is believed to have been as a landmark indicating the entrance to the harbour, which otherwise would have been invisible from the sea. It is the sole remaining witness to the emperor's great naval base and to the trophy of Mark Antony's ignominious defeat which it once held. Unless of course, far below the dancing butterflies and scarlet poppies, relics of one of the most romantic disasters in naval history may still lie preserved deep in the alluvial mud.

Augustus' second visit to the Province was eleven years later—a much longer stay, from 16 to 13 BC. The political landscape had greatly altered in the intervening period. The civil war was over: Augustus was now the unchallenged ruler of a great empire. After the turbulence of the earlier decades peace had settled on Roman lands. In the Province it was time for the consolidation of power, for tightening the reins of administration, and of course for lavish displays of self-aggrandisement. Augustus was supremely adept at all of these.

A number of monuments directly related to this second visit by Augustus have survived. One of these is in a city soon to become especially favoured by the Roman emperors. This was Nîmes, known then as Nemausus, so-called after a sacred spring worshipped by the Celtic tribe which had founded the town several centuries earlier. The famous spring round which the original Celtic settlement had been built flowed out of a hillside immediately to the north of the new Roman town in the valley below. As a mark of the emerging importance of the town Augustus decided to make use of this lofty vantage-point when planning an elaborate cordon of ramparts to encircle the town. Little of it survives today, except for what must always have been its most prominent feature: a massive tower, now known as the Tour Magne, constructed at the highest point of the hill and commanding a lordly view over the town and the entire surrounding area. Like many a tall building in any era, the Tour Magne was erected for status as much as function. Here, presiding over a landscape of conquered lands as far as the sea, was a statement of naked and vainglorious imperial power. Excavations and repairs to the tower were undertaken in the 1970s. It had hitherto enjoyed something of a charmed life: in the seventeenth century there had been a failed attempt to pull it down, following a gnomic predication by Nostradamus that a treasure was concealed within it.

Augustus had another reason for remaining as long as three years in the Province beyond that of streamlining the local administration and spreading the cult of his own godlike magnificence. The great road linking Italy with Spain, begun by Domitius more than a century earlier, was now in the process of completion with the addition of a second arm extending from the Rhône eastwards along the coast into Italy. This was the Via Aurelia, a vital artery for the rapidly expanding trade with Gaul, as well as for the movement of troops. The road needed to hug the sea at the point where the southernmost slopes of the Alps—the Maritime Alps—virtually dip into the Mediterranean. For the Roman powers this precise point presented a serious hazard, particularly to merchants and traders whose passage to and from the Province was under the constant surveillance of hostile bands lurking in the caves and forests within a stone's-throw of the coastal road.

Augustus decided on a full-scale military campaign to subdue the entire region. Though in general peace now reigned throughout the Province, this borderland region of the Maritime Alps had never been effectively colonised and placed under Roman rule. It had remained for the most part an area of independent tribes, partly-nomadic and occupying isolated mountain valleys and sub-alpine pastures. While not persistently hostile to the Roman presence nearby they were not averse to enjoying easy pickings from the caravans of merchandise and new

The Tour Magne at Nimes before its reconstruction. Built as part of the town's defences by Augustus, its plundered condition was the result of a prediction by Nostradamus that a great treasure was buried there.

wealth now beginning to pass along the coast between Italy and the Province.

Augustus possessed no outstanding qualities as a military commander, but his generals did, among the most able being his stepson Tiberius, who was to become his successor as emperor. The Roman armies duly mounted an offensive lasting several years, systematically subduing large areas of the Alpine region, not merely in the Maritime Alps but northwards as far as what are now Switzerland, the Tyrol and Bavaria. Even by Roman military standards it was a hugely ambitious exercise. The result, as recorded bluntly by the Roman historian Cassius Dio, was that 'the Maritime Alps were reduced to slavery.'

La Turbie: the Trophée des Alpes

Forty-five Alpine tribes were crushed in this campaign. That we know the precise number reduced to slavery, as well as their names, is due to the most grandiose commemorative monument of the Augustan era in the whole of the Province—or at least what survives of it. This is the Tropaeum Alpium, the Trophée des Alpes, one hundred and sixty-four feet high, erected on a southern spur of the Maritime Alps in what is now the small town of La Turbie overlooking the Mediterranean and the Riviera far below. The huge monument consisted originally of a rectangular base, or podium, on which the names of the forty-five tribes were inscribed in gold. The precise wording of the inscription has come down to us thanks to the Roman writer Pliny the Elder, who transcribed it half a century later. The monument, he explains, was dedicated 'to the Emperor Augustus Caesar', under whose 'leadership and auspices all the Alpine tribes from the mountains to the sea have been brought under the power of the Roman people.' There followed a list of all the conquered tribes.

Disregarding the certainty that all forty-five tribes would have preferred to be left in peace, in purely military terms to have controlled such a huge mountainous area was an awesome achievement. And in its original state the gigantic monument erected to celebrate that achievement would have been equally awesome. Resting on the podium with its golden inscription rose a circular colonnade. This was surmounted by a steep cone of a roof; while at the very top—as was to be expected—stood a statue of the triumphant Augustus Caesar, at twenty feet high almost four times life-size (Augustus himself being a modest 5 foot 6 inches).

Caesar and Caesar

The hill-town of La Turbie, inland from the Riviera, with the remains of the Trophée des Alpes, erected by the Emperor Augustus to commemorates his victories over the Alpine tribes.

Today what survives of the Trophée has the appearance of a giant decayed molar, capped by a small section of the original colonnade. The cone of a roof has gone, and so has the giant statue of Augustus. In the early eighteenth century, during a war between France and neighbouring Savoy, King Louis XIV ordered its destruction for security reasons—somewhat mysteriously, it might seem, except that the monument then lay outside the borders of France and was no doubt seen as a strategic military outpost. In the event the attempt to blow it up failed: none the less the hapless Trophée soon became a free-for-all quarry, and the local church was built of it along with much of the surrounding village. Finally, what survived the pillagers was tidied up at the beginning of the twentieth century, excavation and repair-work continuing until the 1930s. Since then motorists choosing the fabled Grande Corniche from Nice to Menton (whether in a white open-top Lagonda with a trumpet of a horn or not) pass right beneath it, pausing to gaze down at the glitter of Monte Carlo and the floating palaces of Russian billionaires far below.

And yet—as so often when we find ourselves gazing at the relics of antiquity—this is when the imagination needs to repair the ravages of

ROMAN PROVENCE

The Trophée des Alpes: all that remains of the original colonnade, which once featured a twenty-foot statue of the Emperor Augustus.

time. Here the local museum in La Turbie offers an invaluable visual aid in the form of a model of the Trophée as it once was. Imagine this model to be 164 feet high, and that it stands not surrounded by houses but entirely alone on a bare spur of a mountain as if it had been dropped here by the gods from Mount Olympus. Behind is the vast mass of the Alps extending north as far as Lake Geneva. In front is the open sea stretching to Africa. And on the pinnacle of this giant edifice stands the new god, the emperor-god. In every direction he is the lord of all he surveys, from the Alps to the north, Italy and the Province to the east and west, and to the south the Mediterranean which by now was entirely enclosed by the emperor's lands. It was the Roman lake.

Victory over forty-five Alpine tribes was a triumph indeed. It was one of the emperor's finest hours, even if the number of tribes was perhaps an exaggeration. It was a triumph that symbolised the man himself. Everything that Augustus bequeathed to the Province as a whole, and which his successors perpetuated down the long centuries to follow, echoes that spirit of supreme and unassailable self-confidence, in which nothing is deemed impossible, and the world can be recast in the image of Rome.

Such breathtaking arrogance has a certain magnificence about it, even while we may be glad that the Roman Empire did not last for ever. We need now to look at how one slice of that empire—Provence—was transformed by the time the Romans had finished with it.

3.

TRIUMPH AND TRIUMPHALISM

The Latin word *gloria* could have been invented for the Roman emperors. Glorification was their supreme ambition: it was the ultimate reward of power—to be treated not just as a leader but as a god. And many of the most striking Roman buildings to survive, in Provence as much as anywhere in the empire, are manifestations of that insatiable hunger for glory.

The culture of triumphalism that was born with Julius Caesar, and practised even more vigorously by Augustus, was perpetuated under their successors virtually without exception. Looking at the remarkable number of noble monuments in Roman Provence it is often impossible to be quite certain under the authority of which emperor they were erected. There is a seamless continuity of *gloria* across the centuries. Augustus died in the year 14 AD (at about the time when in Jerusalem the young Jesus was debating with the doctors in the temple and going 'about my Father's business'). Augustus was succeeded by his stepson Tiberius, who was followed less memorably by Caligula until the latter was murdered; then by Claudius (likewise murdered) and Nero (who committed suicide). A procession of lesser emperors steered the empire towards the second century, after which the truly substantial figures of Trajan and Hadrian were followed by Antoninus Pius and Marcus Aurelius—Antoninus Pius being the first Roman emperor to be a native of the Province, having been born in Nemausus (Nîmes).

Many of the large-scale monuments and other grandiose architectural features in the Province were undertaken, or completed, during the reign of those two emperors, Antoninus Pius and Marcus Aurelius, during the second half of the second century AD. This was a prolonged era of peace and prosperity before the renewed barbarian invasions to come—the *Pax Romana* was enjoying one of it better moments—and energies and resources could be expended on the pleasures of life rather than on defence and survival; so, by the end of the century a high pro-

Antoninus Pius, second century AD, the first 'local' Roman emperor, born in Nîmes. (Hermitage Museum, St. Petersburg)

portion of the Roman buildings we now see in Provence and Languedoc were already in place.

By this time, too, the major towns of the Province, all of them relatively young, would have had encircling ramparts of some sort. Few of these survive except in sections here and there, either because towns were constantly expanding due to growing population and prosperity, or because fortifications were a convenient source of building material once defensive walls became of lesser importance. Often only key buildings have remained, in particular town gates which continued to have a valuable function long after the ramparts of which they had formed a part were pulled down. Forum Julii (Fréjus) possesses a number of tantalising fragments including the remains of two monumental gates which once connected Augustus' great naval port to the Via Aurelia, leading to Italy in one direction and to Spain in the other. And on the way to Spain the same road passed through Arelate (Arles) by way of the Porte d'Auguste, likewise a lone survivor of the town's original ramparts.

Further west still, across the Rhône, the road became the Via Domitia, passing after a short distance through Nîmes. Here too are a few scattered survivors of early fortifications. Augustus Caesar is said to have constructed the town's ramparts, almost four miles in length all told, at his own expense. The extent of the fortifications is an indication of the rapid expansion of the town, soon to become the largest in the whole of Roman Gaul. The most prominent survivor of the emperor's fortifications is the massive watchtower known as the Tour Magne (described in the previous chapter), which is among the oldest surviving Roman buildings in France. Besides the tower there are two fragments of the monumental town gates, the Porte de France and the Porte d'Auguste, the road thus threading through the town from east to west before heading towards Spain.

Town gates and watchtowers wear the look of a conqueror's pride and triumphalism far exceeding their defensive function. They are expressions of Roman *gloria*, designed to impress and overawe the visitor—which they still do. At the other end of the scale the same air of celebration and pride of conquest is present in the earliest coins (or possibly medals) to be struck in Nîmes at the time of Augustus' first visit to the Province. The face of these coins shows the head of the emperor alongside that of his right-hand-man and governor of the colony, Marcus Agrippa. But the reverse of the coins bears the cryptic double-image of a palm-tree and a chained crocodile. As so often with fragments of antiquity there is more than one interpretation of their meaning: in this case a prosaic explanation and a romantic one. The former, generally favoured by scholars and offered in guide-books, is that the palm-tree and crocodile refer symbolically to Egypt, and were chosen as the appropriate emblem of Nîmes in honour of the Roman military veterans who were settled here by Augustus after a successful campaign in that country.

The romantic explanation is more poetical, but also more sinister. It is that the emblem is a symbol of the victory of Augustus (or Octavius as he still was) over his greatest rival Mark Antony at the Battle of Actium in the eastern Mediterranean. Antony's headquarters had been in Egypt in the company of his lover the Egyptian Queen Cleopatra—who is therefore not Shakespeare's 'serpent of old Nile' but the 'chained crocodile', whose power, and power over Antony, Augustus had successfully crushed. The image of Agrippa next to that of the emperor on the face of the coins then takes on an extra significance, since as Augustus' general it was Agrippa who had brought about the defeat of Antony and Cleopatra at Actium. This was the ultimate triumph for the emperor-to-be in the Roman civil war.

As for Augustus' relations with the two of them, his letters to Antony in the days when they were still on good terms express strong disapproval at what he considered to be the latter's promiscuous way of life—to which Antony offered a spirited reply: 'Do you object to my sleeping with Cleopatra? ... Does it really matter where, or with whom, one performs the sexual act?' And yet after Cleopatra's suicide Augustus brought her two children by Antony back to Rome and brought them up as his own. Chained crocodile she may have been, yet her legacy remained with him all his life.

An inescapable feature of Roman civilisation, in Provence as much as anywhere in the empire, is the passion for monuments. Roman leaders, from emperors to generals and provincial governors, rarely lost an opportunity to celebrate an achievement, or a key event, in the grandest possible manner. And nothing could be grander than a monument. The Emperor Hadrian even erected a monument to his favourite horse, Borys, when it died at what is now the Provençal town of Apt.

Triumph and Triumphalism

Predictably the grandest form of monument created by the Romans was the triumphal arch. It is the ultimate symbol of military prowess, at the same time proclaiming with a blast of trumpets the arrival of the most superior civilisation on earth, as the Romans never doubted it to be.

Some of the earlier triumphal arches in the Province are relatively modest, at least in size if not in subject-matter. The one at Cavaillon, on the east bank of the River Durance, was erected about 10 BC and consists simply of two free-standing arches like a pair of hoops, both of them decorated with delicate scrolling and leaf-patterns. It was moved to its present site in the square on the edge of the town in the nineteenth century, having originally stood in the very centre at the point where two Roman roads crossed. Then, with the advance of Christianity a cathedral became its close neighbour, gradually swelling in size and importance over the centuries until the diminutive arch was in danger of being elbowed out altogether, whereupon the authorities took the precaution of shifting it stone by stone.

The arch at Carpentras, a short distance north of Cavaillon, is very similar except that the twin side-panels have survived; and the power-

The triumphal arch at Carpentras, featuring carvings of 'barbarian' captives in chains. The arch was long used as an entrance porch to the local Gothic cathedral.

ful carvings on each side reveal exactly what the triumph was about. The best-preserved of the panels shows two chained figures of 'barbarian' captives, one of them dressed in animal skins, standing on either side of a tree hung with victors' trophies, the trophies being the weapons of the captives. The bald statement of conquest, and the air of contemptuous superiority which accompanies it, could not be clearer. And yet there is a crude strength in the way the figures are carved, and a formal dignity about the whole scene, which lift it far above the customary display of triumphalism. In all, the Carpentras arch remains one of the lesser-known masterpieces of Roman sculpture in Provence; yet it is likely to have survived only because the city's massive Gothic cathedral was built right next to it, and the Roman arch once served as a useful entrance porch.

A different case of re-employment relates to a triumphal arch even less widely known than that of Carpentras. This is in the ancient town of Die, a former Celtic stronghold in the hilly region far to the north of present-day Provence. Why the Emperor Augustus should have chosen to transform such a remote Celtic settlement into what became a prosperous Roman town is only made clear by locating Die on a map, and noticing which river passes right below it. This is the Drôme, the most important river to bisect this region east and west, and therefore a vital thread of communication: furthermore the Drôme eventually flows into a river vastly more important still, the Rhône, which was the principal artery for the transport of commercial goods in the whole of southern Gaul. Merchants travelling westwards from Die would join that great river at a point conveniently halfway between two major Roman towns, Vienne to the north and Orange to the south. No wonder Augustus found it worth his while to subdue a small Celtic citadel, and to crown that success with a triumphal arch—which has survived to this day because, more than a millennium later, it was given a new and practical function, one it still enjoys, as a handsome entrance gate to the town.

To the east of the great artery of the Rhône, and following the course of it northwards, ran another major Roman highway, known as the Via Agrippa, so-called after the most outstanding of Augustus' generals, and his close friend and adviser, Marcus Agrippa. It was on this new highway that a Roman colony was established about the year 35

Triumph and Triumphalism

BC, and some years later the grandest of all the triumphal arches in Provence was erected there. This was—and still is—the great arch at Orange. Seventy-two feet high, and sixty-nine feet wide, it straddles the ancient Via Agrippa on the northern edge of the town like some ageless pachyderm turned to stone, scoured by that relentless north wind, the mistral, yet still an enduring witness to Roman glory.

Like other Roman towns in the Province—Narbonne, Arles, Nîmes and Fréjus—Orange was a colony created by veteran soldiers who were settled here, and given land, as a form of pension in reward for military services to Rome. In this case the settlers were soldiers of the Roman 2nd Legion who had served in Gaul, so the territory they were awarded had formerly belonged to the native Celtic tribe they had conquered, and were now displaced (who knows where?) in the customary fashion. The new colony was known as Arausio, after a Celtic god of springs—the name being all that remained of the unfortunate former inhabitants. (At a later date the word Arausio became confused with that of a citrus fruit, so becoming Orange.)

The gigantic arch was built by the new settlers to commemorate the victory which had given them their new home. The carved panels

Witness to Roman glory, the great triumphal arch at Orange, straddling the Via Agrippa heading northwards.

on both sides depict scenes of that military triumph, including the trophies of armour and jewellery, even the name of the defeated tribal chieftain, Sacrovir, which is engraved on one of the captured battle-shields among the customary display of chained prisoners being led to slavery. The stirring impact of the arch must have been greatly enhanced when originally it was surmounted by the triumphant bronze sculpture consisting of a war-chariot drawn by the four prancing horses of a *quadriga*.

There has been wide disagreement about when exactly the Orange arch was built. Guidebooks make matters no clearer by offering dates of either around 20 BC or 20 AD, so inviting the assumption of a typographical howler somewhere. But not so. It could have been either date, or later still. Reason may suggest the earlier of the two is the more likely, since this would be in the lifetime of many of the original veterans with their memories of hand-to-hand combat with the Celtic tribesmen and even the name of their chieftain. If so, it would place the arch in the years immediately following the first visit of Augustus Caesar to the Province. Alas, we know that the arch was actually dedicated not to the Emperor Augustus but to his successor the Emperor Tiberius in 27 AD, which naturally suggests the arch may have been built (or partly rebuilt) in the immediately preceding years—unless of course the citizens of the now-flourishing colony were indulging in a display of political sycophancy, keeping in with the new ruler and benefactor by dedicating their triumphal arch a second time. Scholars have wrangled for centuries over the matter, and will certainly continue to do so for as long as the great arch stands.

The presence of Tiberius in the Province is more shadowy than that of his two mighty predecessors. He succeeded Augustus in 14 AD, and reigned for a further twenty-three years. A good many of the Roman monuments that were begun under Augustus would have progressed further, or been completed, under Tiberius. It was a period of relatively peace in the Province, and of expanding trade and prosperity. There was time and money for lavish building. Yet the dedication of the Orange triumphal arch to Tiberius raises a further puzzling question. If the dedication was truly in 27 BC, Tiberius by this time had long abandoned his successful military career and was in the process of retiring from Roman political life altogether, in favour of prolonged sojourns in the

Triumph and Triumphalism

Campania and finally semi-retirement on the island of Capri. Suetonius in his *Life of Tiberius* records that the emperor became increasingly paranoid during his island retirement, and recounts lurid tales of sexual perversions and moral depravity in general. Tacitus in his *Annals*, his last great historical work, offers equally sickening accounts of the old emperor's indiscriminate acts of cruelty towards suspected enemies. 'Executions were now a stimulus to his fury,' he writes. 'There lay, singly or in heaps, the unnumbered dead... until they were dragged to the Tiber where, either floating or driven to the bank, no one dared to touch them.' In another passage Tacitus adds his verdict: 'Finally he plunged into every wickedness and disgrace, when fear and shame being cast off, he simply indulged his own inclinations.'

In all, it seems unlikely that the Roman citizens of Orange, in dedicating their great arch to such a ruler, are likely to have received much in reward.

One further passage by Tacitus. in the *Annals* (Book 15), recounts the most momentous event in the emperor's reign: this is the bald statement that 'Christus' was convicted by Pontius Pilate during the reign of Tiberius. It is scarcely more than a footnote; not an event considered to be of much importance, certainly not worthy of a triumphal arch. Tiberius' own footnote in history is far more deeply engraved: in Christian eyes he was the Roman ruler under whose imperial authority the son of God was crucified.

One place in Provence today captures more dramatically than anywhere else in the region the glamour and the mystique of Roman monuments, and that is the area a short distance to the south of St.-Rémy known as 'Les Antiques'. The 'antiquities' are a pair of monuments, a triumphal arch and a mausoleum, and they stand isolated among scattered pine-trees against a backdrop of the Alpilles whose jagged peaks jab at the sky in this most theatrical of settings. In the dry heat of midday the monuments can seem to shimmer as if they were images in a mirage transported here from some other place or time. And as we walk towards them we are greeted by a deafening fanfare of cicadas from the surrounding trees.

ROMAN PROVENCE

If the whole area evokes some surprising memories this may be because we have indeed seen it all before—those pine-studded hills, the walled cornfields, the stark cypresses, the gnarled olive trees, the orange farmhouse roofs: they are vividly familiar because Van Gogh painted them all during the year he spent here as a voluntary inmate of the asylum and former monastery which still stands a few hundred yards from the two Roman monuments. Strangely, though he must have seen them every day Van Gogh never seems to have painted them, which is puzzling since he painted just about everything else around him during that frenzied year so close to his own death.

But then he never painted the great Greco-Roman city of Glanum either, the ruins of which spread out from here as far as the cleft in the mountains beyond. In this case it was for the simple reason that the existence of the place was still unknown and unexcavated at that time. All Van Gogh would have known of Glanum was the nearby quarry from which it had been built (and which he did paint).

St.-Rémy de Provence: the Triumphal Arch

The triumphal arch of St.-Rémy was once the noble entrance gate to the lost city. By the end of the first century AD most Roman towns of any size had entrance gates which tended to double up as triumphal arches. Civic pride and national glory marched happily together. The St.-Rémy arch is one of the earliest in Provence, dating from the reign of Augustus early in that century. Unlike the monument in Orange this has one arch, not three. It has also lost much of its superstructure, possibly when Glanum itself was sacked and destroyed by Germanic tribes in the third century, or when the local people, having been evicted, were rebuilding their town a little to the north and took advantage of so much available stone. In its shorn state the arch had one further contribution to make: it was to inspire the main portal of one of the finest mediaeval churches in Provence, St.-Trophime in Arles, a short distance to the west.

The St.-Rémy arch was originally part of an extensive boundary wall, and in its pristine state would have been a symbol of the city's splendour at the time of Augustus. It also carried a familiar message. Two surviving carved panels on either side of the arch depict the usual cluster of chained Gallic prisoners personifying the subjugation of Gaul by the

Triumph and Triumphalism

'Les Antiques' near St.-Rémy de Provence: the mausoleum (left) and the remains of the triumphal arch which was once the entrance to the city of Glanum.

Roman conquerors, and hence offering a grim warning to those who might still be contemplating revolt. The carvings are badly weathered, but not so severely that they obscure the unexpected poignancy of the scene. Most carvings of this theme on other triumphal arches are scarcely more than propaganda statements, impersonal and dehumanised, pointing a conqueror's finger at the folly of rebellion. Here the two pairs of figures are life-size and painfully human, in particular the pair on the right of the arch. They are of a man and a woman. He is chained, and being dragged from her. She turns her head away, weeping, a hand raised to her face. He will become a Roman slave. Who knows what will become of her? None the less this *is* a triumphal arch, and the Roman message cannot be far away. The right-hand panel shows yet another Gallic prisoner, this time with a boy—his son?—who wears a cloak draped in the Roman fashion. In other words, the younger generation at least have seen the light.

Taken together, the two panels transcend the usual cold triumphalism we have come to expect from such carvings. For once they are more than propaganda, and they come as a surprise: they are proof that the

ROMAN PROVENCE

At the side of the St.-Rémy triumphal arch, a chained Gallic prisoner dragged from his wife and led away into slavery.

conquerors could sometimes unbend and portray the tragic price the defeated had to pay at their hands. This is close to being great art; and if less damaged might have been so. All too little Roman sculpture possesses such a touching gift of compassion.

One explanation for such unexpected humanity is that the workshop responsible for these carvings may well have been Greek. Glanum, though originally Celtic, had been a Greek city—an offshoot of Massalia—until the relatively recent Roman takeover, and the Greek cultural influence would still have been strong. Just as in the Roman world Greek was still the written language of the intelligentsia, so the most powerful tradition in Roman stone-carving was the example of the great classical sculptors of the Hellenic world. The likelihood of the St.-Rémy figures being Greek, at least in inspiration, is strengthened by the ornamental frieze of carved leaves, fruit and flowers which runs like a decorative ribbon round the outside of the arch itself, with an enchanting lightness of touch that is unquestionably Greek.

Triumph and Triumphalism

The second of the two St.-Rémy monuments standing guard outside the ruins of Glanum is more of a puzzle, and has bred some imaginative interpretations as to who and what it was designed for, and precisely when. The monument is generally known as the St.-Rémy mausoleum, and it is either a tomb or a cenotaph depending on your view of its function. Beyond doubt is that it was built to honour the dead, and hence was erected on the edge of the Glanum necropolis, or burial-ground. Unlike the triumphal arch nearby it is virtually undamaged, making it hard to realise that it is actually more than two thousand years old: and this uneasy sensation is further aggravated by the fact that the mausoleum became the model for modern cenotaphs honouring the dead of two world wars.

In appearance it is a series of small buildings stacked one above another. On a rectangular stepped base rests a square podium faced on all four sides by carved friezes illustrating mythological scenes—a cavalry charge, a battle with Amazons, a boar-hunt and a fight between Greeks and Trojans. The panel on the north face includes a Latin inscription, which is the main source of passionate dispute about what the monument is all about. Above the podium sits a four-sided arch flanked by fluted columns with Corinthian capitals, and a keystone carved with a Gorgon's head, the symbolic guardian of the tomb. Finally the top layer comprises a circular temple (or *tholos*) of further

A battle scene: one of the panels round the base of the St.-Rémy mausoleum.

Corinthian columns within which stand two carved figures wearing togas whose identity has been yet another fertile breeding-ground of speculation.

The Latin inscription on the podium offers the only clue to the purpose of the monument. It translates as 'Sextus. Lucius. Marcus. Sons of Caius of the Julius family. To their forebears.'

One can be tempted to believe that inscriptions are sometimes worded deliberately to mystify future generations and thereby ensure that their authors would never be forgotten. And this inscription is a case in point. So, who were these three brothers? And the Julius family? Which forebears? And why should the tomb be dedicated to them? The key signpost here is the family name, Julius. This was of course the family name of Julius Caesar. And it is this apparent link with Caesar's family which has inspired a long-held conviction that the forebears alluded to in the inscription were indeed Julius and Augustus Caesar, whose statues are then the two carved figures near the top of the monument. Augustus, after all, had been adopted by Julius in his will as his son and heir, and was therefore entitled to the family name. As to the three brothers, the names of two of them, Caius and Lucius, corresponded neatly with those of Augustus' adopted grandsons (who were later killed in Syria and Spain in 4 and 2 AD respectively).

This interpretation, with its clatter of big names, would make the monument not a tomb but a cenotaph erected simply in honour of a celebrated father and grandfather.

Alas, scholarship can be unkind to dreams. There is now general agreement among cognoscenti that the St.-Rémy mausoleum is considerably earlier than the triumphal arch next to it, and can hardly have been built later than 30 BC. At a stroke this rules out any possibility that the brothers responsible for the dedication could have been Augustus' grandchildren since they may not even have been born. As for the name Caius, supposed to be their father, we know that the real father of Augustus' grandsons was the emperor's celebrated general and personal friend, Agrippa, whose forenames were Marcus Vipsanius, not Caius.

The likely true story of the monument, and the inscription which adorns it, is very different and rather poignant. It is indeed a tomb, not just a memorial. The three brothers are playing tribute to their dead forebears who are buried here, and are represented by the two statues

Triumph and Triumphalism

high up in the circular *tholos*. What appears most plausible is that the father and grandfather were not Romans but natives of Gaul, most likely of Glanum itself, who had been recruited into the Roman army at some early stage and had both distinguished themselves conspicuously in Caesar's Gallic wars. As a reward for their outstanding services they were granted Roman citizenship and awarded the special privilege of being allowed to take on one of the most prestigious family names in the Roman world, that of Julius, or the Julii. This at least is now the received wisdom.

The inscription and the monument itself offer a more benevolent view of Roman conquest than the usual unrelenting triumphalism. It becomes necessary here to understand that in the eyes of Rome the civilisation which the conquerors imposed upon native peoples was so infinitely superior to any other that it entirely justified their actions, however cruel and overbearing that might appear to be. And all was not necessarily grim for the conquered. Those among them who cooperated with the invaders and did well could be handsomely rewarded, like the family responsible for the St.-Rémy mausoleum. If there is a foretaste of British India here, and the anglicising of the Indian professional classes, then the comparison is not misplaced if not pressed too far. The impenetrable self-righteousness of power was common to both empires.

If this reading of the St.-Rémy inscription is correct then the Julii family of Glanum are golden representatives of a new colonial elite society. Under Roman rule Glanum, like many other Roman towns, had been granted the status of *Oppidum Latinum*, soon to be elevated to that of a 'colony'. These privileges boosted the prosperity and importance of the town, and facilitated the advancement of respected local families like the Julii, already crowned with battle honours, to attain positions of civic and political authority as representatives of Rome. They were quite possibly descendants of the defeated Celtic tribesmen who had first built the town round its sacred and healing spring. Now Roman citizenship gave them a huge social lift. They were now the *nouveaux riches*, and it was families like them who became responsible for the Roman town whose ruins survive today, spreading out into the valley between the hills. They were the people who built, embellished and enriched the place.

One of the dynamic enterprises of the people of Roman Glanum—

though we have no idea whose brains and engineering skills lay behind it—was the construction of a great dam across a valley to the west of the town, built in a long row of reinforced arches. In the nineteenth century a new dam replaced it, and only tell-tale incisions in the flanking rocks have enabled archaeologists to reconstruct a faithful mental picture of it. The dam is believed to be the earliest of its type ever known, dating from about the time when the Julii family were erecting the St.-Rémy mausoleum, and its purpose was to store water for the new town brought from the nearby Alpilles hills by means of an aqueduct.

But the story of aqueducts, and the Roman engineering genius for all aspects of hydraulics, is for another chapter. In the context of Roman triumphs, this was perhaps their greatest.

4.

THE ARCHITECTURE OF WATER

The most precious commodity in any society is water; and a strong case can probably be made out for the most successful societies having been those which possessed the skills for controlling and utilising the supply of it—whether in a flood zone, a desert, a rain-forest, sub-arctic tundra or our gentle temperate climate suitable for cows and hens.

How the Romans score in such a broad evaluation is not hard to assess. By any measure they possessed a genius second to none for making water do precisely whatever they wanted it to do, whether it was fountains, baths, irrigation schemes, water-mills or mock naval battles in flooded amphitheatres. In the process they often seemed to defy the laws of nature, employing techniques that were at least a millennium ahead of their time. Water became the Romans' obedient servant: and it served them well.

They were by no means the first to understand how a natural supply of water could be re-directed for the benefit of human beings. Without gazing further afield than the Mediterranean region and the Middle East we can trace effective hydraulic systems in Ancient Egypt during the Old Kingdom four thousand years ago. The Egyptians had the benefit of the Nile on their very doorstep, which makes the achievement of the Persians roughly a thousand years later the more remarkable. They invented a system of allowing gravity to draw water underground from the mountains in order to irrigate the arid plains by means of a long chain of wells known as *qanats* (still in use in Iran today and clearly visible from the air like tracer-bullet trails crisscrossing the desert). The earliest Greek aqueducts were likewise underground: one water channel on the island of Samos dating from the sixth century BC is said (though it sounds highly exaggerated) to have been tunnelled through a mountain for the best part of a mile to bring water to the island's principal town.

The Romans began to construct their own aqueducts about two

A genius for channelling water. The early aqueducts round Rome and in Roman Provence inspired spectacular engineering feats throughout the empire, like this aqueduct in Segovia, Spain, a century later.

The Architecture of Water

hundred years later. The first of these, towards the end of the fourth century BC, was built to the south of Rome in conjunction with the new paved highway, the Via Appia, and consisted of nothing more sophisticated than an extended covered trench some fifty feet deep. Engineering science then took a giant step forward: by the middle of the second century BC Rome was being served by an aqueduct, the Aqua Marcia, which was constructed above ground by means of a line of tall stone arches. It was to be the first of many. And the modern aqueduct was born.

It was the Romans' mastery of the arch—how to cut, shape and lay stone so precisely that it could bear enormous weight—which turned water engineering into one of the key factors in their phenomenal success, both domestically and as empire builders. Being able to direct water to wherever they needed it meant that cities could flourish and expand, and food be produced for their inhabitants and livestock. Water was the means of survival and of prosperity, as well as a source of pleasure and of public hygiene. Before long giant aqueducts served virtually every city in the empire. They straddled the conquered lands as well as their own, from Europe to the Middle East to North Africa. Aqueducts were the hallmark of Rome's utter supremacy.

The Roman occupation of Provence, Languedoc and the other areas which together made up the Province took place only a few decades after the first arched aqueduct had been built in Rome, towards the end of the second century BC. It was as a result of that successful campaign in southern Gaul that these new engineering skills were able to be developed and to expand; and this breakthrough came about—like so many achievements in the Roman world—through military necessity. The first great Roman general, the legendary Caius Marius, made the decision on arrival in the region to create a permanent standing army to combat the repeated threat of attack by Celtic and Germanic tribes, hastily-assembled armies having proved disastrous. While waiting to engage those tribes in what was to be the decisive battle (described in Chapter 1) Marius employed his men as a labour force to dig a vital canal linking his military camp to the naval port which he had established. The Fos canal no longer exists except for a few disconnected threads of water; yet this was the waterway that became the precursor of any number of future engineering projects, offering proof to the

Roman authorities that soldiers could play a secondary role almost as valuable as fighting barbarian tribesmen. The story of Roman engineering owes a great deal to the foresight of Caius Marius.

As the historian Sallust commented a few decades later, Marius had the good sense to recruit soldiers from all walks of life, particularly from the proletariat. As a result his army was composed of men with a wide variety of practical skills. This soon became a tradition in the Roman army. And over the course of the following centuries that standing army which Marius had instituted incorporated many of the finest engineers and skilled craftsmen in the Roman world, with an array of ambitious building projects and public works placed in their capable hands. Furthermore, as a body of men they could receive handsome benefits. In addition to these civic duties, as fighting men they were also rewarded by whatever they could manage to pillage. Then, once retired from active service they could be awarded the lands they had conquered. In all, then, the life of a professional Roman soldier posted to serve in the Province can hardly have been a prison sentence.

Much of our knowledge of early Roman engineering projects and techniques, particularly in relation to aqueducts, comes from the writings of the architect and military engineer, Marcus Vitruvius, a figure universally known because of an iconic drawing by Leonardo da Vinci, *Vitruvian Man*. Vitruvius wrote the first treatise on architecture in the Roman world: this consisted of a collection of ten books entitled *De Architectura*, composed during the first century BC and dedicated personally to the Emperor Augustus, who seems to have been his benefactor.

Vitruvius is particularly illuminating on the theme of water engineering, which had become the key science of the day, and his views on the subject have a beguiling freshness and charm thoroughly unexpected in the midst of a weighty treatise on architecture. On how to detect the presence of water underground he recommends, 'Just before sunrise lie face downwards on the ground, resting your chin in your hands. Take a look over the countryside: where you see vapour curling up from the ground you will find water if you dig.' And on spring-water he is equally confident: 'If the spring is free-running and open, look at the people who are dependent upon it: if they are strong, have fresh complexions and clear eyes, then the water is good.'

The Architecture of Water

As a man who relished the natural world Vitruvius was insistent that architecture itself should be an imitation of nature, and of natural forms: hence any structure needed to possess the qualities of 'durability and usefulness', but it should also be 'beautiful'. These were enlightened views which must have owed much to the Greeks, whose architecture he deeply admired. His thoughts had a particular application to aqueducts, which in his eyes obeyed these strictures; and his descriptions of how aqueducts were constructed, and what materials should be used, are especially apt since Vitruvius was writing at exactly the time when some of the finest Roman aqueducts were being built, both in Italy itself and in the empire, including of course the Province.

One line in Vitruvius' writings brings vividly to mind the most elegant of all Roman aqueducts, 'The channel should be covered over in order to shield the water from the sun.' We can see the result of that advice in the form of a stone roof covering the entire length of that supreme masterpiece among Roman aqueducts, the Pont du Gard. And for many centuries the principal water supply for the city of Nemausus (Nîmes) flowed beneath that stone roof.

※

We do not know if Vitruvius ever travelled to what is now Provence. What we do know from his own writings is that as young man he served in the Roman army under Julius Caesar, possibly therefore in the Gallic Wars: in which case it is not unlikely that he may have come here. Whether as a military engineer he may even have played some small part in the Pont du Gard being constructed, or simply been aware of its existence, is even more speculative. Unfortunately we know next to nothing about Vitruvius' life except what he tells us in his treatise. As for the Pont du Gard, much as we would love to know its full history, we find ourselves in the midst of another of those scholarly disputes which occupy a great deal of space in print but have no agreed resolution: in this case—when precisely, or even imprecisely, was it built?

What at least is beyond all such dispute is that throughout the centuries the Pont du Gard has been widely recognised as the largest and the greatest of all Roman bridges. It has been universally seen as an example of engineering raised to the level of a work of art. Plaudits for it are legion. In the mid-eighteenth century the Scottish author Tobias Smollett visited it and later recorded the effect it had made on him in his *Travels through France and Italy*. It was, he claimed, 'a piece of architecture so unaffectedly elegant, so simple and majestic, that I will defy the most phlegmatic and stupid spectator to behold it without admiration.' He went on to fantasise that he longed to dive under one of the arches on a summer evening—a dream acted out today by appreciative visitors every day. Early in the nineteenth century the French novelist Stendhal, after completing his first masterpiece *Le Rouge et le Noir*, ventured south to gather material for a book to be entitled *Travels in the South of France*. The Pont du Gard rendered him almost speechless: it stirred him, he wrote, 'like some sublime music'. Half a century later that indefatigable Victorian journalist and traveller Sir Theodore Cook asserted in his book *Old Provence* that 'the builders of the Pont du Gard… seem even today to have been the agents of some greater power than the world had seen before.' In our own time Lawrence Durrell in his musings on Provence, *Caesar's Vast Ghost*, claims 'it is not possible to look upon those great mortarless arches without emotion. They are hymns to the Goddess of Water.'

Few people visiting the Pont du Gard today are likely to quibble over these sentiments.

The Pont du Gard

Putting the great bridge in its geographical context, the Pont du Gard forms part of an extended channel built to bring water to Nîmes from the hills immediately to the north. The distance from the source to the city was only twelve miles as the crow flies: but there were major physical problems to be overcome which made a direct route out of the question. The most outstanding of these problems was that at some point the channel would need to cross a rugged valley through which the River Gardon flowed.

An accompanying problem—and an even more testing one—was the gradient. The difference in altitude from the source of water to the city itself was a mere 56 feet: hence the slope allowing the water to flow freely would have to be extremely shallow along its entire length; and in order to maintain this slope any crossing of the Gardon would need to be by means of an exceptionally high bridge. There was only one place

The Architecture of Water

The Pont du Gard, which supplied water to Nîmes. The accompanying road bridge in the foreground, now closed, was added in the eighteenth century.

along the entire length of the valley where the land on either side was high enough to make such a bridge possible, and that was some distance to the east. This inevitably stretched the line of the channel into a dog's-leg, extending its length to almost three times that of the direct route: 35 miles instead of twelve. The extra distance also meant that the gradient had to be even shallower: the hydraulic engineers needed to calculate a drop of no more than seventeen inches per mile, an exercise that would require minute precision in the laying of each stone slab. And since the channel also needed to follow the twists and turns of the high ground on both sides of the river in order to keep the necessary gradient, sometimes even tunnelling through bare rock for stretches of almost 200 feet, precision just as minute was needed by the surveyors as they mapped out every foot of those 35 miles.

Equally remarkable were the skills of the architect and stonemasons who actually built the giant bridge. The Romans had mastered the art of building stone arches capable of bearing immense weight; but this bridge needed to be far higher than could be achieved with a single row of arches. The solution was to erect three bridges one above the other. Six foundation arches were built to span the river itself, each set wide enough

ROMAN PROVENCE

The magnificent Pont du Gard, spanning the River Gardon in the course of a 35-mile journey to Nîmes, maintaining the necessary drop of no more than seventeen inches per mile.

to allow floodwater to flow freely between them. Eleven arches with more slender piers formed the second layer; while the top layer was built of thirty-five small arches, with the precious water channel running on top of it, roofed over with hefty stone slabs just as Vitruvius had recommended.

And so, with this ingenious three-tiered construction the height required to maintain the necessary gradient was achieved. It was an extraordinary achievement.

The stone used for the bridge came conveniently from a quarry (recently still in use) only a mile away near the village now called Vers. Some of the stone segments needed to be of a colossal size for weight-bearing purposes, themselves weighing up to six tons. Precise measuring and cutting of each block was crucial since they were all laid without mortar or metal clamps: they were hauled into position by means of winches operated by enormous wooden wheels, and held in place—for two thousand years—purely by gravity. The expertise of the masons even included the nicety of realising that blocks of cut stones weathered best if laid the same way up as when they were quarried. A complex system of scaffolding was used, and the protruding stones used to hold it are still visible today.

The Architecture of Water

Considering the rudimentary tools and equipment at their disposal, it is impossible not to be astonished at the combined skills of surveyors, architects, stonemasons and hydraulics experts. Here was an enterprise so demanding and intricate that it would have stretched the ability of engineers right up until the Industrial Revolution.

The route of the great water channel to Nîmes can for the most part still be followed. The actual source of water consisted of a number of springs in the area of what is now the town of Uzès, some of them now buried under the town itself. Early in the last century underground workings are said to have revealed elaborate drainage systems and a huge well at least fifteen feet in diameter. From these springs water was then channelled, as it is today, along the low-lying and verdant Eure valley. To maintain the required shallow gradient the channel needed to be kept on higher ground; and south-east of Uzès it was carved through naked rock to avoid a lengthy detour. Along the same stretch it bridges what must have been a small stream, and a short distance further on a crumbling section of aqueduct has survived in the scrubby terrain, consisting of 35 arches. Then comes the Pont du Gard itself, after which the route bends sharply westward in the direction of Nîmes, tunnelling through further outcrops of rock before crossing and re-crossing a modern road and a motorway running parallel to it.

The point of arrival at Nîmes: the *Castellum Divisorium*, from where water was piped to different areas of the city.

Precisely where and how the channel finally reached Nîmes at the end of its 35-mile journey was unclear until the mid-nineteenth century. Then excavations in the midst of building operations revealed an elaborate stone basin, circular in shape, with a large square inlet. This would have been the end of the channel. Known as the *Castellum Divisorium*, today it is shielded by high walls and cypress trees—a private shrine to the water-gods. The stone basin has a low rim in which ten cylindrical holes have been bored, radiating outwards. And from every hole lead pipes would once have re-directed water to different parts of the town— to fill public baths and water-troughs, operate fountains which the Romans loved, and serve important public buildings and the houses of civic dignitaries; while at the foot of the basin three further openings allowed excess water to flush the town's sewers. The Romans knew about public hygiene as well as hydraulics.

The entire undertaking—the long aqueduct, the elaborate system of water distribution and especially the great bridge itself—is a monument to Roman engineering genius.

It would be rewarding to know that it was also a monument to a man of extraordinary gifts and vision. But here the dark clouds descend. Who *was* responsible for this huge enterprise? Who did design and build the Pont du Gard? At least we know who was responsible for defacing it. During the French wars of religion in the sixteenth century the Duc de Rohan cut away a third of the thickness of the entire second tier of arches so that his cannons could cross the river over the first row of arches. It remains a tribute to Roman building skills that the Pont du Gard survived the duke's assault. Then, to add insult to injury a new bridge—today's road bridge—was constructed in the eighteenth century along the eastern flank. The combination of these adjustments and additions weakened its structure, until by the mid-nineteenth century only careful renovation averted serious danger of the aqueduct collapsing altogether. In 1958 it survived a major flood which destroyed modern bridges in the region, since when further restoration has been carried out under the auspices of UNESCO. Today an informative visitor centre, landscaped approaches to the site and occasional spectacular *son- et lumière* events add to its popularity during the tourist season, when swimmers and canoeists mingle in the river under its vast arches.

The long-cherished view of who was responsible for the Pont du

The Architecture of Water

Gard is that it was the brilliant general and close friend of the Emperor Augustus, Marcus Agrippa—hero of the Battle of Actium and destroyer of Mark Antony and Queen Cleopatra. And if it was indeed Agrippa who masterminded the great bridge, then it would probably have been during the second of his two periods as governor of the Province, around the year 19 BC.

The attribution to Agrippa can be traced to the Roman historian Suetonius in his *Life of Augustus*. Claiming that Agrippa was responsible for 'a variety of magnificent buildings', he recounts the story of how Augustus answered public complaints about the rising price of wine with the assertion that Agrippa's aqueducts were more than sufficient to quench everyone's thirst (thereby roundly m missing the point). It seems that the great general, when not commanding the Roman armies in battle, was responsible for supervising Rome's water supplies and sewage system, including the designing of the city's aqueducts. So, given that he also became governor of the Province, it seems a reasonable assumption that he might have been responsible for the Pont du Gard during his governorship. Furthermore he is known to have made generous gifts to Nemausus; and since his close friend and colleague was the wealthiest man in Rome, the eponymous Gaius Maecenas, there would have been no shortage of funds for sponsoring an engineering project on this scale designed to bring water to the city he loved. Finally, as a general he would have had the Roman army stationed here entirely at his disposal. The work-force and expertise required for building the mighty bridge would have consisted (apart from slaves to do the dirty work) of soldiers, many of them highly skilled men in different areas. The permanent standing army introduced by Marius nearly a century earlier existed for precisely such a purpose whenever there were no wars against barbarian tribes to be fought.

By putting together all these disparate pieces Agrippa easily becomes a strong candidate for the role of architect and overseer of the Pont du Gard. And as such he has received accolades in plenty, most recently from Lawrence Durrell. Describing the viaduct as 'Agrippa's great stone bauble', Durrell goes on to admit to 'feeling a sudden keen wave of curiosity and awe about Agrippa if you find yourself standing at sunset on the great stone plinth of the Pont du Gard, which together with the magnificent Pantheon in Rome is the handiwork of this prodigious and enigmatic personage... He was more than just an engineer mesmerised by the functional attributes of his stonework... His eye was that of a superb artist with a lust for fine stone and a profound feeling for the stress engendered by the passage of water in its canals.'

But scholarship, as so often, spoils the party. The received wisdom today is that the Pont du Gard was not even built during the reign of the Emperor Augustus; hence Agrippa could have played no part in it during his period as governor, or later (since he died shortly afterwards).

The favoured date is now the mid-first century AD, which places it less appealingly in the reign of the psychopath Caligula. Yet not every expert agrees, and the dispute rumbles on. It may be that the giant structure was indeed designed and begun under Agrippa's governorship, but never completed until half a century later. As to the identity of the architect, a small clue is offered by the name 'Veranius' engraved on one of the arches of the second tier. Yet anyone responsible for a construction quite as splendid and as daring as the Pont du Gard would surely have made his presence known more proudly than this.

The undying magnificence of the Pont du Gard overrides all such dreams and speculations. It remains, beyond debate, one of the wonders of the ancient world.

※

If the Pont du Gard remains the most spectacular of all Roman aqueducts, there are many others in the region which still catch the eye as they stride across the Provençal landscape. To the east of Nîmes the sister-city of Arles also received its water supply from the hills: in this case from the jagged peaks of the Alpilles, further east still. Most of the long aqueduct has disappeared, and there is no equivalent of the grandeur of the Pont du Gard to grab our attention. Water entered Arles in a tunnel beneath one of the city's gates, the Porte d'Auguste, and was then redirected, as in Nîmes, to different parts of the city including the great amphitheatre.

The most intensive construction of aqueducts took place further north in the Rhône Valley, beyond the boundary of present-day Provence. The great river itself was an obvious source of local water, but dramatic changes in water levels in different seasons, and often severe

The Architecture of Water

flooding, made it unsuitable for serving aqueducts. Springs were a more manageable source, and most of the towns on the Rhône, Vienne in particular, received their water supply from the mountainous regions on either side, the Ardèche to the west of the river and the Drôme to the east, where rainfall was often heavy and the flow of water along the aqueducts steady and constant.

No fewer than eleven Roman aqueducts have been identified in the northern area of the Rhône Valley in the region of Vienne. Four of these channelled water from a range of low mountains to the west of Vienne known today as the Monts-du-Lyonnais. And the name is apt: all four aqueducts supplied water for a former Gallic-Celtic settlement which Julius Caesar had captured and which Agrippa later made the capital of the Province at the time he was governor. It was a place which enjoyed huge strategic importance, sited at the junction of two major rivers, the Rhône as it flowed south-west from Lake Geneva and the Alps, and the Saône flowing southwards from Burgundy. The new Roman town was Lugdunum, which has come down to us as Lyon.

By the second century AD it had expanded greatly, as the need for four aqueducts suggests. Remnants of all four have survived, the best-preserved being the Gier aqueduct: this took water from a stream in the Monts-du Lyonnais and delivered it to Lugdunum 54 miles away

The longest aqueduct in Roman Provence, at Gier, north-west of Vienne, which supplied water to Lugdunum (today Lyon).

to the north-east—more than half as long again as the Nîmes aqueduct, and requiring twenty-five bridges across rivulets and ravines. Here was another engineering feat that was challenging even by Roman standards. Much of the Gier aqueduct was an underground channel, but one stretch above ground which has survived in the suburban outskirts of modern Lyon, called the Arches de Chaponost, consists of no fewer than ninety arches and covers a distance of nearly half a mile: the longest and best-preserved stretch of Roman aqueduct in the whole of France.

Besides discovering how to divert and channel water the Romans also learnt how to contain and store it. They built dams. Our knowledge of their dam-building is limited largely because dams, unlike aqueducts, have tended to be replaced as engineering skills in hydraulics have advanced. The Alpilles dam near Glanum, mentioned in the previous chapter, is a case in point. Since the construction of a larger dam in the nineteenth century scarcely any traces of it have survived barring a few marks in the rock-face. Yet this was an impressive piece of engineering consisting of a long row of reinforced arches. A similar story surrounds a dam which may have been even more impressive in that it was constructed to trap water from the great mountain to the east of Aix, Montagne Ste.-Victoire. The dam was built over a gorge near what is today the small town of Le Tholonet (in the heart of Cézanne country), its purpose being to hold water from a fast-flowing stream which gushed down the north face of the mountain. Unlike the Alpilles dam there is at least concrete evidence—even if tantalisingly little—of the massive construction that was once here, in the shape of a formidable chunk of masonry buried like a lost dinosaur in the midst of some of the wildest terrain in Provence. Again all else has vanished, replaced in the mid-nineteenth century by the Barrage Zola and, further upstream through gorges and dense woodland, the more recent and huge Barrage de Blimont.

Amidst these vast enterprises the Romans also saw to it that fresh water was available for everyday use even in relatively small communities. The tradition of the village fountain, which soon became the ubiquitous village pump, is one of the abiding legacies of the Roman Empire. There are many such fountains in Provence, and until recent times they were the only source of fresh water available to the inhabitants. How

The Architecture of Water

many of them date back to Roman times is not always easy to establish; but one notable village near the coast can claim two fountains which unquestionably date from that period. The village is Ceyreste, a short distance inland from the port of Le Ciotat, which was originally a Roman town, to the east of Marseille. One of the fountains is merely a hole in the wall by the roadside: but the other has a more folkloric look—a large stone basin in the centre of the village covered over by a heavy protective roof shaped like a miniature bridge.

Further east along the coast are the remains of one of the most daring feats of Roman water engineering in the Province. This is the extended viaduct which brought fresh water to the port and naval base of Forum Julii, now Fréjus, founded by Julius Caesar and greatly expanded by Augustus. The length of the channel from the hills to the sea is roughly 25 miles, which is shorter than the Nîmes aqueduct; and neither does it incorporate a structure quite as magnificent as the Pont du Gard. None the less the Fréjus aqueduct was an equally demanding test of hydraulics skills, and the terrain to be surveyed even more demanding.

The channel began close to the hilltop village of Mons (to the west of Grasse). The village itself is perched on a high cliff above the valley. And at the base of the cliff a spring gushes out and becomes a small river called the Siagnole. The Roman engineers began their water channel here. They were immediately confronted by the same hazard their predecessors had encountered near the Pont du Gard, the need to hack through solid rock in order to keep the required gradient. The cutting—still relatively unchanged amid the scrub of the hillside after nearly two thousand years—was 165 feet long, the central section being a tunnel carved through the hill. From here the channel maintained its perilous course southwards, sometimes underground, sometimes arching over ravines and rivers, in a landscape that could hardly have been less friendly to water engineers using primitive equipment operated by an army of slaves. Some of the taller arches were supported by sloping buttresses, an indication of the strength of the violent west wind, the mistral; but also suggesting that building skills had advanced since the Nîmes aqueduct built at least a century earlier. Finally the channel skirted the Massif de l'Esterel, hugging the valley of the Reyran on its way towards the coast. Today the landscape through which it passes is

ROMAN PROVENCE

Remains of the aqueduct bringing water 25 miles from the hilltop village of Mons to the port and naval base of Forum Julii (today Fréjus).

in many areas spotted with modern villas and in one place traversed by the Riviera motorway. More than a hundred years ago the indomitable Sir Theodore Cook explored the entire length of the channel, concluding 'I can conceive of no more interesting journey than one, with a good guide, which follows the whole line of the arches.'

The most impressive section of the aqueduct which survives today forms the dramatic centrepiece of an immaculate tree-lined park in Fréjus itself. The setting could not be more unlike the hostile landscape in which the aqueduct was originally built, or even the landscape familiar to Sir Theodore relatively recently. A line of elephantine arches stretches across well-watered lawns and flower-beds, their reddish stone set against a vibrant Riviera sky. Roman engineering has become an open-air stage set: except that it has proved to be more permanent than the modern world around it. In December 1959 the Malpasset dam, constructed across the Reynan river-valley close to the aqueduct some miles inland, burst and flooded the whole area, destroying parts of Fréjus and killing 400 people. Despite the tragedy the Roman aqueduct survived.

5.
The Soil and the Sea

Under Augustus Caesar the Province began to prosper. Or at least its Roman conquerors certainly prospered, and it is reasonable to suppose that a proportion of that affluence seeped down through the ranks of the native Gallic population. Their leaders would in any case have become thoroughly Romanised by now, enjoying the privileges which came with their elevated status, the most coveted being Roman citizenship. Gaul, and the Province in particular, was in the process of being absorbed by Rome.

The *Pax Augusta* which the emperor's iron hand imposed upon his expanding empire may not have allowed much breathing-space for his subject peoples, but it was exceedingly good for trade. Merchants could travel in relative safety, and farmers take their goods to market with less fear of being robbed. Law and order had huge commercial as well as personal advantages. Augustus himself was an outstanding organiser, and the efficiency of his administration made an impact right across the empire, from regional government down to local markets and trade routes. Roman historians and commentators—Plutarch, Martial, Strabo and above all Pliny the Elder—all remark on the rich and varied produce of the land in Roman Gaul, the Province in particular. There was a flourishing trade in wine, oil, cheese, figs and wheat: there are also accounts of extensive mining of iron, copper, silver and gold. And as a measure of this new prosperity villas and luxurious spas were springing up across the Province, and virtually every town now boasted its own aqueduct bringing fresh water from the hills.

Outside the towns the population by and large was not grouped in villages—a relatively modern concept. Instead country people in the Province tended to live and work in scattered farmsteads which were small communities in themselves: they were self-sufficient economic units made up of the landowner and his extended family, attended by a varying number of slaves who acted as servants and did most of the physical work on the land under the master's supervision. These compact farming communities were generally known as 'villas'. And although luxurious mansions with fountains and elegant colonnades certainly did exist they were the exception, the rare perquisites of extreme wealth and idleness to match: by and large the Roman villa was more of a small working hamlet, not unlike the tight clusters of farmhouses forming single units which are still a feature of the more isolated areas of rural Provence.

Farming in the Province was transformed by the Romans in a number of ways. Crucially, ownership of the land shifted from local Gallic tribes to the conquerors. Even the concept of 'ownership' was novel, since many of the Gallic tribes whom the Romans encountered were semi-nomadic, moving their flocks and their dwellings according to the seasons or the promise of fresh pastures. Of the large number of veteran soldiers from the Gallic Wars who were now awarded land as a form of retirement pension, many took advantage of their bonus by becoming farmers, either displacing whoever happened to be there or re-

An indication of farming wealth: amphorae for storing oil and wine. Many of the new farms were settled by retired Roman soldiers given land as a pension.

ducing them to tenants and labourers. In addition, the prospect of land-for-free attracted many opportunist Romans from Italy to come and grab whatever they could lay their hands on in the conquered territories. Furthermore, the running of these newly-acquired farms was greatly facilitated by the availability of slaves, many of them former rebellious tribesmen who had been defeated by the very Roman soldiers who were now their masters. In fact agricultural prosperity in the Province was to a considerable extent the product of the slave society which the Romans had created.

Disregarding the ethics of this Roman land-grab, the new shift of ownership contributed enormously to increased efficiency in farming, and in trade generally. Towns we now know as Narbonne, Nîmes, Arles and Vienne had become flourishing centres of trade. The Rhône was busier than ever as an artery conveying goods north and south, while along the coast Marseille, still a Greek city though under Roman authority, remained the most important of a number of ports in the Province shipping produce to and from Italy as well as elsewhere in the Mediterranean.

One indication of the region's growing prosperity was the flourishing trade in wine. In the early days of the Roman conquest there seems to have been an Italian monopoly of wine production, imposed as a protectionist measure by Rome and clearly indicated by the quantity of Italian amphorae which have survived. (Every museum of antiquities in Provence today seems to have its own rich collection of such vessels in which foreign wine was once imported.) Wine had been made locally long before the Roman invasion. The Greeks who founded the port of Massalia around the seventh century BC are known to have introduced wine-grapes and wine-making to the region, and there is evidence that long before the arrival of the Romans they were enjoying a trade in wine with Gallic tribes further north by means of the River Rhône. The Roman historian Justinius pronounced that 'from the Greeks the people of Gaul learnt a civilised way of life'. By the first century AD a great deal of local wine was being produced, not only around Massalia but in the region of Béziers and Narbonne to the west, and Vienne in the Rhône Valley. Now it was even being exported to Rome in ever-increasing quantities, as we know from the existence of amphorae found in Italy with the proud declaration 'Five Years Old'.

There survives one disapproving comment—which has a distinctly modern ring—about the additives which the wine-makers of Narbonne chose to mix with their wine in order to enrich its colour and flavour. The complaint was amplified by an alarming list of the actual substances commonly used. The author would certainly have known what he was talking about since he is a primary source of information about agricultural methods in Roman Europe, as well as about many other aspects of Roman daily life. He was Gaius Plinius, generally know as Pliny the Elder: and his masterwork, *Historia Naturalis*, all thirty-seven books of it, he completed in the year 77 AD.

Pliny never lived to enjoy the acclaim which his huge work of scholarship was to attract. Two years later, in the summer of 79 AD, there was a massive eruption of Mount Vesuvius. A fleet of Roman ships was anchored close by in the Bay of Naples, and its commander was none other than Pliny. His appointment was the latest in a successful public career that had seen him as a cavalry commander, proconsul in Gaul, legal adviser in Rome and the holder of several lofty official posts under successive Roman emperors. The eruption of Vesuvius was witnessed by Pliny from his ship as a menacing black cloud which rose and spread outwards in the shape of a giant tree. With his fascination for everything to do with the natural world he could not resist going ashore to see for himself what the phenomenon might be, and what damage it was causing.

There may also have been personal reasons for his decision to go ashore. He owned a villa close by in which he was now spending much of his time in semi-retirement. In addition, the area close to Mount Vesuvius, in particular the land round Pompeii, was at that time a major wine-growing region and a principal source of supply for Rome itself. In fact the wealthy merchants of Pompeii were infamous for drinking to excess, a habit on which Pliny comments wryly, prompting him to make his celebrated pronouncement: *in vino veritas*.

In the event his curiosity cost Pliny his life. Poisonous fumes overcame him before he could return to his ship. We owe the account of the disaster to his young nephew and adopted son, Pliny the Younger, who described it in a letter to his friend in Rome, the historian Tacitus. And so it transpired that the historic eruption which buried the cities of Pompeii and Herculaneum also accounted for one of the world's first

The Soil and the Sea

great naturalists, and the first knowledgeable commentator on the wines of Roman Provence.

It may be that the destruction of the Pompeii vineyards by the eruption of Vesuvius contributed to the huge increase in the export of Provençal wines to Rome during the last decades of the first century. Pliny had already reported, before the eruption, that some wines from the Rhône Valley were fetching high prices in Rome, particularly those flavoured with pine resin (so dispelling any conviction that *retsina* is a uniquely Greek creation). By and large, though, for the citizens of Rome the Province was the source of cheap 'plonk'. And it is not hard to see why. Land in the Province was free, and so was slave labour. Many of the Roman soldiers who had been awarded land as a retirement pension seized the opportunity to become farmers; and in any case some of them are quite likely to have been the sons of wine-growers back in Italy. So, in order to satisfy this new and lucrative export market they set about planting out the virgin hillsides around Narbonne and Nîmes, creating what are believed to have been the very first large-scale vineyards in France.

Pliny points out that the area which soon became the centre of the wine trade in the Province was the Rhône Valley, with Vienne as the principal local market. The advantages of Vienne were multiple. The sheltered slopes on either side of the Rhône lent themselves admirably to the growing of wine-grapes (as they still do), and from here barges could convey wine vessels southwards down the Rhône and the Fos canal to Massalia for shipment direct to Rome; but also up-river to another market that was equally important because it served the entire central and northern Gaul as well as the rest of northern Europe. This was Lugdunum, now Lyon.

In all, Vienne catered for a prodigious amount of Roman thirst in just about every direction.

Inevitably, unlike the aqueducts, temples and amphitheatres which dominate the landscape, there are few surviving witnesses to the immensely successful wine industry in Roman Provence. There are of course amphorae galore. And there are delightful vignettes of grape-

A delightful relief carving of river transport on the Rhône with the aid of ropes, and an oar as a rudder. (Musée Lapidaire, Avignon)

picking and wine-quaffing around the borders of large floor mosaics. Of particular charm is a carving in low relief now in Avignon's Musée Lapidaire but originally from a Roman villa. It depicts a vessel laden with goods being steered by a man in the stern while other figures (no doubt slaves) are hauling the boat upstream with stout ropes. Here was wine being transported up the Rhône, or its tributary the Durance, to the markets of Vienne or Lyon—just as we can imagine hundreds of such vessels regularly braved the swift currents of the great river in the interest of those far-flung legions and Romanised tribesmen who by now had developed a taste for the grape almost as robust as that of Pliny's merchants of Pompeii.

Among the many preferences and recommendations made by Pliny was the suggestion that vines should be trained up trees or high pergolas, in the manner of some of the finest grape-vines in the Roman Campania. Pliny went on to warn that the practice could be dangerous, and labourers should make sure that their contract with employers guaranteed meeting the cost of a funeral. Training vines in this Roman fashion was probably never common in the Province on account of the infamous mistral; yet there is one remarkable estate where the practice has been revived. A short distance to the west of the Rhône, between Avignon and Arles, is a large and handsome farmhouse called the Mas des Tourelles (meaning 'towers'). It dates from the seventeenth century, but beneath it and in the surrounding grounds have been found traces of an extensive Roman villa and estate dating back to the first century AD, with evidence of wine-production on a large scale, as well as an accompanying pottery where the storage jars were made. On the strength of this discovery the proprietors of the *mas* set about recreating the original estate as faithfully as possible. As a result, ignoring the erosion of time, we find ourselves becoming visitors to a Roman farm at the very time when Pliny was writing about such places. Those who choose to volunteer may even find themselves scaling trees and pergolas to pick the grapes, treading them with bare feet, or manning a gigantic wine-press which is weighted by an entire oak-tree laid horizontally and operated by a battery of levers and pulleys.

The equipment and precise working methods employed at the Mas des Tourelles derive from a Roman authority who was writing a full two centuries before the time of Pliny, and to whom Pliny would certainly have owed a great deal. He was a Roman statesman and scholar by the name of Marcus Porcius Cato (also known as Cato the Elder), and in the mid-second century BC he composed a treatise on farming entitled *De Agri Cultura*, which has the added distinction of being the oldest surviving complete work of prose to be written in Latin. More to the point, the work became the required textbook for Roman winemakers in Roman Italy, and continued to be so for many centuries to follow.

Cato's treatise was composed several decades before the first Roman soldiers set foot in Provence. None the less its enduring fame makes it more than likely that those retired military veterans who became farmers, and who planted out the first vineyards here to the west of the Rhône, would have had access to Cato's textbook and his words of wisdom. Hence the giant wine-press in the Mas des Tourelles has been designed strictly in accordance with Cato's instructions. Hence too the design of the garden and the accompanying vineyards, which includes an area with vines trained up pergolas and trees. This was exactly as Pliny recommended; though Cato was offering the same advice long before Pliny—on the somewhat puzzling grounds that since grape-vines need as much sun as possible they should be encouraged to climb up trees.

The Mas des Tourelles opens a window on to the lost world of Roman agriculture. In its day this estate would have been one of many in the Province. And, doubtless like others, it would have been established precisely where it is for one strategic reason, At the edge of the estate, beyond the garden and the vineyards and the site of the pottery, runs a by-road whose only distinction is that it is bordered here and there by large granite slabs. These are described as *bornes militaires*: they are boundary markers, some of them milestones, and they are witnesses to the fact that this quiet by-road is a section of the former Via Domitia. In other words this handsome estate was within a stone's-throw of the great Roman highway which, besides its military function, was the principal trade route running east and west across the Province, to Spain in one direction, to the Rhône and Massalia in the other. The Mas des Tourelles could hardly have been better placed.

For a Roman landowner the alternative to having a working estate next to one of the new paved highways was to establish it close to a navigable river. To the east of the Rhône runs a broad tributary which joins the main river near Avignon. This is the Durance: and a short distance from where it joins the Rhône, at Caumont, is another recent recreation of a former Roman estate. Unlike the Mas des Tourelles this was never a commercial set-up but a lavish pleasure garden created for some dignitary at the time of Augustus Caesar who must have been exceptionally important as well as exceptionally wealthy.

As so often with important archaeological sites the Roman estate at Caumont was discovered by chance through excavations for new building works. What was revealed was the basic structure of the largest Roman ornamental garden in the whole of France. Much of it was made up of eight separate areas, each dedicated to one of the Roman gods—Jupiter, Apollo, Minerva, Bacchus and Diana among them—each planted out with trees and plants representing aspects of the life and mythology of the respective deity. The garden was nature's shrine to the gods, and to ancient mythology in general, since it included a full-scale labyrinth in honour of Theseus and the Minotaur. Accompanying these elaborate exercises in botanical symbolism was a pool 215 feet in length in which the master of the villa could bask while contemplating the blessings which those gods had showered upon him. Today, strolling among the fruit-trees and the scented herbs we may find ourselves overtaken by a different thought, that but for far-sighted management by local authorities and private speculators this enchanting corner of paradise would now be a building-site.

In terms of Roman utilisation of the land nothing could be further than Caumont from olive-picking in the Provençal heat, or the

The Soil and the Sea

manning of giant pulleys to operate a felled oak-tree as a wine-press. We are in a land of sybaritic pleasures, not toil.

Those Roman veterans who settled down after the Gallic Wars to become farmers seem to have concentrated by and large on a few lucrative crops. Besides grapes, two other fruits were much in demand: figs and, above all, olives. As with the wine-grape, it was the Greeks who had introduced the olive, originally a native of what is now mainland Turkey. The Greeks who founded Massalia around 600 BC came originally from that area. They brought with them the olive (probably the fig too), which they proceeded to plant and grow locally, and very soon in their extended territories along the coast as well as their inland settlements such as Glanum and Theline (later Arelate, and later still Arles).

By the time the Romans arrived in the region nearly 500 years later the olive had long been established; and since olive trees are famously long-lived, the first Roman soldiers to reach the area may well have encountered plantations already five centuries old. (There is even reputed to be an olive tree near the hill-village of Roquebrune, close to Menton and Cap Martin, which may have been planted at the time of Augustus Caesar two thousand years ago.)

Farms such as the one re-created at the Mas des Tourelles certainly cultivated olives as well as vines. Olive oil was valuable for lamps, but above all for cooking; and during the seven years of the Gallic Wars the demand for it multiplied. Supplies were conveyed northwards up the Rhône in sealed earthenware jars to wherever Caesar's armies were encamped. Production of oil in the south was further encouraged by Julius Caesar's successor, Augustus, and before long there was evidently a healthy export trade to Italy, however much this may sound like 'coals to Newcastle'. Proof of such a trade is provided by a chance discovery in Marseille during reconstruction work near the Vieux Port after the Second World War. Warehouses related to the old Greek and Roman docks came to light containing quantities of amphorae and other storage vessels for both wine and olive oil. Today this revelation of Marseille's long trading history has become the Musée des Docks Romains.

To the west of Marseille across the broad Etang de Berre, on a rocky spur half-hidden among pine-woods, is an evocative site which even in its wrecked state speaks of another local industry which flourished long before the Romans arrived. The place now bears its Christianised name, St.-Blaise, and the industry which once flourished here by the huge lake was salt.

There is a certain mystery about this place. It was always, so it would seem, a centre for the production and dispatch of sea-salt, which would have been dried and scooped up along the edges of the *étang*. The first occupants of the site were probably the Etruscans, who built a trading-post here as early as the seventh century BC. When the Greeks arrived and created the larger trading port of Massalia the Etruscans appear to have departed, leaving the settlement for the Greeks to expand and to exploit the exceedingly lucrative salt trade. This they did so successfully that between the third and first centuries BC the St.-Blaise site extended to half a mile in length on two levels overlooking the lagoon. Its ruins are still there as an eloquent witness to past affluence

But at this point the mystery thickens. Archaeological evidence shows that the site endured a violent siege, whether by a local tribe such as the Salyens or by the newly-arrived Romans is unclear. If it was the latter then it remains equally unclear why a settlement so long prosperous should shortly afterwards decline and, apart from a short-lived recovery in the first century AD, should eventually become totally abandoned for several hundred years. Another partial recovery took place during the final decades of Roman rule, and the settlement met its final destruction at the hands of the Saracens a few centuries later.

The fluctuating fortunes of St.-Blaise remain particularly puzzling since throughout the six centuries of Roman occupation salt was among the most precious commodities of the age. In Italy a special salt road was constructed to supply the Roman armies in the regions further north. One answer to the mystery may be that the production of sea-salt in the lagoons close to Massalia had become impractical compared to other areas. And here one strong candidate emerges, only a short distance to the west: the Camargue.

The saltwater marshes of the Camargue extend for almost fifty miles along the coast. And the salt industry here is long-established; in the Middle Ages the product was so valuable it was referred to as 'white gold'. There can be no doubt at all that the Romans established salt-pans here—the *salins* as they are called now—in which the level of seawater could be controlled and allowed to dry out during the hot summer

The Soil and the Sea

months, leaving the crystallised salt ready to be raked up and transported by barge along one of the many veins of the Rhône. (It was the ever-changing delta of the great river, combined with continual invasions of the sea, which had created the wilderness of the Camargue.)

The first documented evidence of a Roman salt industry here is none the less surprisingly late, not until the fourth century AD. We know that an engineer by the name of Peccaius was appointed by the Roman authorities in nearby Arles to be in charge of salt production in the region. It is not recorded precisely what his methods were, yet his name has survived for seventeen hundred years in several locations within the Camargue. A small settlement, an ancient tower and, above all, a canal still bear the name Peccaïs. With so enduring a name it seems reasonable to suppose that Peccaius may have systematised the Camargue salt industry, perhaps laying out the grid-pattern of salt-pans which remain a feature of the industry today. Maybe, too, the mediaeval salt road which led northwards from the marshes to Nîmes at the time when the early monasteries controlled the industry owes its origin to Roman times and the organisation of Engineer Peccaius.

The fickle geography of the Rhône delta—river-floods, shifting water-courses, invasions by the sea—has destroyed most evidence of Roman activity in the Camargue. Yet we know that many of the veteran

A modern-day salt mountain near the coast in the Camargue. The Romans developed the lucrative industry of evaporating sea-water in open pans, then raking the salt up to dry. Salt became known as the 'white gold of the Camargue'.

soldiers whom Julius Caesar settled in the region of Arles established villas here and became farmers. The very name 'Camargue' may well derive from one such Roman landowner by the name of Aulus Annius Camars who owned a large estate. A marble inscription in his honour is on display in the Musée de la Camargue (eight miles to the southwest of Arles). And according to Julius Caesar's *Commentaries* there was one outstanding reason why Roman farmers occupied themselves so profitably in the delta. This was the cultivation of corn—on a scale so large that Caesar described the area as being the granary of the Roman armies in Gaul. There can be no doubt that, inland from the saltmarshes, the soil of the Camargue was rich from thousands of years of silt deposited by the Rhône as it regularly flooded the land. An unexpected tribute to the quality of the local soil is a fragment of a stone statue also in the Camargue Museum. The carving depicting the Roman god of farming, Priapus—the guardian of forests, rivers and fields—whose renowned gift of fertility is most frequently represented by his sexual organ of 'priapic' proportions (here long since removed: maybe now a rare collectors' item). Judging by the quantity of the grain the soil regularly yielded the Roman farmers of the Camargue had every good reason to thank their well-endowed god for his benison.

Pliny, so often the sharpest eye-witness to Roman agricultural practices, was also the first writer to mention an optimistic invention in Roman Gaul which may possibly have contributed to the prodigious success of arable farming in Provence generally, and particularly here in the Camargue. This was a machine dating from the time of Augustus Caesar which was a rudimentary form of reaper called a *vallus*. From the few relief carvings showing this contraption it appears that it was pushed by hand, probably with the aid of a donkey suitably harnessed, with the rotating blades somehow depositing the cut corn into a large open box. Until then corn had always been reaped by hand, usually by slaves using a form of scythe or sickle. Whether the *vallus* was actually in use here is uncertain. In any event productivity was soon so high that a *procurator* was appointed by the authorities in Arelate to purchase locally-grown corn for dispatch by barge to the Roman armies; but supplies had become so plentiful that quantities of grain were also regularly shipped down the Fos canal to the sea and thence to Massalia to be shipped direct to Ostia, the port of Rome.

The Soil and the Sea

The Province was now in a position to supply the capital of the Roman Empire itself.

The Barbégal Watermill

Another Roman invention, one that was infinitely more daring and imaginative than the primitive *vallus*, is today one of the most dramatic features of the Provençal landscape some six miles to the east of Arles: a place known as Barbégal. It is also among the least-visited of the major archaeological sites in the region, largely because nobody visiting it without prior knowledge is likely to have the faintest idea what it is.

It begins with an aqueduct, or rather the remains of one, like a row of broken teeth protruding from the summer grassland and the olive groves. It is not obvious where the aqueduct comes from, or where it is leading, except that it is heading south. Eventually the line of crumbled arches approaches a wall of bare rock, and at this point a deep cleft opens up some twelve feet deep and wide enough to walk through with a few feet to spare on either side. At first there appears to be nothing beyond the cutting in the rock except the sky. Then comes the surprise: emerg-

The ruins of the Barbégal watermill. Sixteen mill-wheels were driven by water channelled from the Alpilles hills—the first known example of industrial mass-production in the western world.

ing from the cutting suddenly the broad plain of the Crau opens up below, extending south-east towards Marseille and south-west to the final stretch of the Rhône and the marshes of the Camargue beyond.

And in the foreground of this vast panorama, immediately below, the stony hillside drops steeply away in a jumble of smashed walls with passages of stone steps among outcrops of bleached rock all the way down as far as the fields at the base of the hill.

It is no wonder that it took archaeologists until the middle of the twentieth century to work out what this place was. The fact that the site had long been used as a quarry for local building contributed to the confusion. However, one clue always remained—the aqueduct leading to it: an aqueduct, what was more, which apparently ended in thin air. Except, of course, it did not end in thin air. The water-course must have continued down the hill. Barbégal, it was finally understood, was a watermill.

Today a detailed model of what the Barbégal watermill would have looked like is displayed in Arles in the handsome new Musée de l'Arles Antique. With this image in mind it now becomes possible to gaze down from the point where the water channel emerges from the hill, and to envisage the lay-out of the mill and how such an ambitious feat of hydraulics was made to function.

The source of water brought here by the aqueduct was the range of rough hills nearly six miles to the north: the Alpilles. In fact the aqueduct performed a dual role: it brought water to Arles, and it operated the mill. Accordingly the aqueduct branched shortly before the cutting in the rock, the western arm (no longer existing) heading towards Arles. The channel which continued through the cleft in the rock then divided a second time and became twin water-courses flowing in parallel down the slope. This double mill-race descended through sixteen separate chambers, eight on either side, each containing a wheel that was turned by the impact of the water, so operating a mill-stone attached to it. The water then flowed on to the next wheel, and the next, and the next, and so on. A broad stone stairway ran between the parallel channels; and here the bags of milled flour were carried down the steps and loaded into barges waiting in the canal below—a canal created by the very water that operated the whole milling process.

The barges' destination was Arles, close of course to the Camargue, where the corn had been grown in the first place—Caesar's granary of

The Soil and the Sea

Remains of the aqueduct conveying water to the Barbégal mill, which supplied flour for the entire city of Arles.

Roman Gaul. It has been calculated that the mill was capable of producing around forty-five tons a day, sufficient for the entire population of Arles, some 13,000 people. When we consider that the same aqueduct from the Alpilles provided the city with its fresh water supply and the flour for its bread, as well as the means of transporting it, then the value of that six-mile stretch of engineering from the Alpilles hills becomes incalculable.

The Barbégal mill has been described as the first example of industrial mass-production in the western world. Whether this is literally true or not, it remains a phenomenal achievement from almost two thousand years ago—sixteen mill-wheels, sixteen mill-stones, all mounted on the side of a barren hill that has been transformed into a double cascade by means of a stone channel bringing spring water from a distant range of hills: the entire operation being achieved with the most basic technology, yet with extraordinary mathematical and practical intelligence. Barbégal is another example of Roman engineering genius.

Major Roman Sites

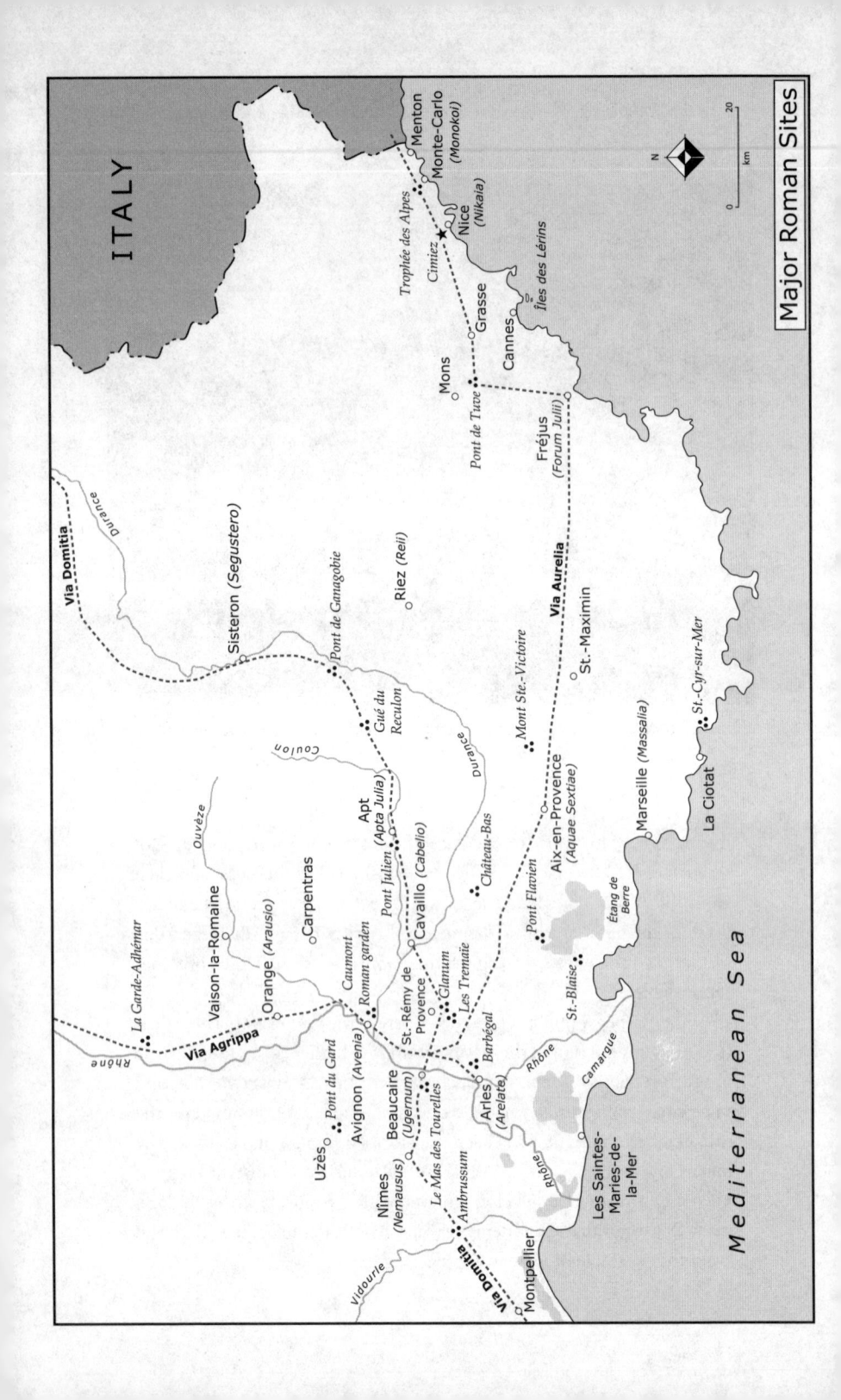

6.
New Cities... and How to Live

The Romans brought urban life to southern Gaul. With the exception of the flourishing Greek port of Massalia and a few neighbouring communities which were spawned by it, town-dwelling was not a practice enjoyed by the native inhabitants of the region. The multiplicity of Celtic and other tribes who occupied the area before the Roman conquest had for the most part lived a rural existence on the land which fed them and on which their animals grazed. The population was widely scattered and often semi-nomadic, with isolated pockets of local authority where chieftains and ruling families maintained fortified settlements which the Romans came to describe as *oppida*, Entremont, on the edge of modern Aix-en-Provence, being a prominent example (see Chapter 1).

Then, from the period of Caesar Augustus onwards the new Roman Province became increasingly urbanised, to a large extent due to the number of veteran soldiers from the Gallic wars who were settled here. It was a way of life modelled on that of Rome itself, each new city becoming conceived as a kind of miniature Rome. Along with the accepted plan of how a city should be built—in the form of a grid—came the notion of central administration. At the heart of the Roman concept of how a civilised life should be led was the conviction that the city must be the hub from which civic authority and decision-making in general radiated throughout the far-flung colonial territories. From the new cities extended the long arm of the law. They were the core of civilisation, the citadel, symbols of Roman insistence on control, efficiency and public order. And how very modern that sounds: Gallic bureaucracy was truly born here.

For the new town-dwellers urban life also brought about an important shift in values and priorities. Instead of mere subsistence-living, a richer and more rewarding way of life now presented itself. Physical comforts, entertainment, leisure activities such as bathing, enjoying public gardens, facilities for sports and gymnastics, massage and health treatments—such pursuits began to become part of the expectation of the new city-dwellers. Not everyone needed to live close to the source of food: in a well-ordered world domestic commodities could be brought to the cities, just as water could be provided thanks to the Roman genius for engineering.

One inevitable result was the creation of a privileged urban elite. The political stability which the Roman presence imposed on the region led to mounting economic prosperity, largely because the Province was strategically placed for trade northwards via the Rhône and southwards to the entire Mediterranean via the port of Massalia. And it was the merchants and entrepreneurs among this new elite class who reaped much of the resulting benefit.

Nor was it only the Romans who basked in this new urban sunshine, enjoying the thermal baths, the theatres and the sporting facilities. Many of the new cities (Nemausus/Nîmes being an obvious example) were expansions of existing Gallic settlements located round holy shrines. They would have been relatively small in size: none the less there was a native population to be accommodated, even if only treated as servants. Furthermore, most of these cities were created (or greatly enlarged) by veteran soldiers given land as a retirement pension, many of whom would have been native Gauls in the first place, having been recruited locally to serve in the Roman legions. It is known that

A statue of a Gaul dressed in a Roman toga, known as the Vachères warrior, c. first century BC. Leading local families became increasingly Romanised, particularly in the towns, enjoying urban life with its attendant pleasures of baths, sporting facilities and entertainments in the new theatres and amphitheatres. They also began to speak Latin rather than their native tongue, and to become literate. They were the new Romans.

New Cities... and How to Live

Augustus Caesar's famous Transalpine legion, the Alauda, contained 5000 Gauls all of whom were granted Roman citizenship on their release from military service. Altogether it seems likely that in these new cities of the Province 'true Romans' were always likely to be outnumbered by 'natives'.

The leading families among these native Gauls became increasingly assimilated into this Romanised life—and not only Romanised, but Latinised. The numerous Celtic and local languages were spoken, not written. The Gallic leaders who became assimilated into Roman life and were awarded Roman citizenship not only learnt to speak Latin, but often to read it and to write it. They became literate. And in doing so they came to belong to two worlds. Cicero described their situation as early as the first century BC: the people of southern Gaul, he claimed, had 'two fatherlands, one of their birth and the other of their citizenship'.

The spread of the Latin language over the various local tongues was a vital contribution to Roman success in the region. Just as Greek had been the language of the educated classes in Rome, so Latin became the language of education throughout the Province. Hence it inevitably became the language of commerce, and of the law (and soon, equally inevitably, the language of the Christian Church). What was more, the new literate elite were naturally city-dwellers, and their presence made the cities of the Province cauldrons of business activity, political debate, much wealth and—most conspicuously—pleasure, of which those new Romans in their new cities became abundantly fond.

The heart of Roman city life was the forum. This was the central square, generally paved, where people could gather to meet friends, conduct business, discuss ideas, engage in political debate, enjoy gossip, hear the latest official pronouncement about taxes and tariffs or simply eye each other and mingle with the crowd. Close to the forum was the seat of local government, and invariably a temple likely to be dedicated to either Jupiter, Juno or Minerva, the three most favoured deities (all of them borrowed from the Greeks). Round the edge of the square would be offices as well as a variety of shops, and these were often roofed over by a portico against bad weather, providing shelter also for beggars, touts, layabouts, prostitutes and any other people of the shadows who found the heart of a Roman city to be a place of rich pickings.

Besides a covered portico the forum was sometimes accompanied by an underground area known as a *cryptoporticus*, the function of which was probably to provide storage space for the various shops around the forum above. The best surviving example is in Arles, dating from the period of Augustus, and consisting of three underground galleries each a hundred yards long in the shape of a double horseshoe, like the letter 'm'. That it was almost certainly used for storing foodstuffs is indicated by ventilation shafts leading up to the forum. One of the most likely uses for this underground warehouse was as a huge granary: and here it brings to mind once again that the nearby Camargue was described by Julius Caesar as the granary for the Roman armies in Gaul. The grain had to be stored somewhere, and the Arles *cryptoporticus* would seem to be the obvious candidate. Then, in the later centuries of the Roman presence we have the evidence of the enormous watermill of Barbégal a short distance to the east of Arles, and which we know milled flour for the entire city (see Chapter 5).

It is not hard to reconstruct a plausible scene in which wheat grown in the well-irrigated fields of the Camargue is harvested in midsummer and brought to Arles where it is stored in the *cryptoporticus* awaiting transportation to Barbégal: then once it is milled the flour is carried back daily to the city by canal barge to be stored in another area of the underground warehouse until being brought up to the bread ovens round the fringes of the forum. It is a harmonious picture of city life the success of which lay in the extraordinary skill which the Romans possessed in making even the most limited of natural resources work for their well-being and, of course, for their pleasure and for profit, at which they were equally adept.

Today Arles has its Place du Forum, but no forum, which in any case lay a short distance to the south. Instead the square which bears its name is given over to that standard-bearer of Provençal language and culture, the Nobel Prize-winning poet Frédéric Mistral, whose statue lords it over the square, eclipsed only by the more universal fame of Vincent Van Gogh, who painted his *Night Café* right here under the gas-lamps and the stars, as a million tourists come to celebrate every summer with a nostalgic *pastis*.

New Cities... and How to Live

Floor mosaic from a private villa in the region of Arles depicting the Greek myth of Europa and the Bull (Zeus). (Musée de l'Arles Antique)

Arles was always important, from the moment when the city fathers made the shrewd decision to support Julius Caesar in the civil war against Pompey, and became showered with privileges as a result at the expense of Massalia, which had supported Pompey. Arles continued to expand in wealth and political importance under Caesar's successor, Augustus (who planned the new city and built its forum). The expansion continued under successive Roman emperors until by the fourth century Arles could be described, by the poet Ausonius, as 'the Little Rome of Gaul'. By now the city was entrusted with the honour of minting imperial money: and in the final decades of the empire, in the mid-fifth century Arles replaced Lyon as the political and administrative capital of the whole of Roman Gaul, an area which included Spain and Brittany besides what is now France. In doing so it became—if only briefly—second in importance only to Rome itself among European cities.

Arles could not have been more strategically placed, at the axis of two key roads, the Via Domitia/Via Aurelia running east to west linking Italy with Spain, and the Via Agrippa which followed the valley of the River Rhône northwards towards Lyon and the markets of northern Europe. The waterways were vital arteries, not only the Rhône but its tributary the Durance, and the canal built by Marius linking Arles with the sea, as well as the lagoons—far more numerous than today—all of which facilitated the transport of a variety of goods to the city, from woollen textiles to gold and silver mined to the west of the region. At the heart of all this local trade were the Arles shipyards which had first flourished when Julius Caesar commissioned a fleet of vessels to be built in his campaign against Pompey. Over the succeeding five centuries locally-built trading vessels were constantly moored in the dockyards along the west bank of the Rhône in what is now the suburb of Trinquetaille, loaded up with goods to be shipped upriver to Lyon and the markets of northern Europe, or down the canal to the sea and eventually to all parts of the Mediterranean.

In order to facilitate access from the city to the Trinquetaille dockyards the Romans constructed the antecedent of the modern pontoon bridge—literally a bridge of boats, flexible enough to withstand the fierce floods and currents of the great river. Naturally enough nothing survives of the famous 'pontoon bridge', though miniature models of it have been pieced together from fragments of evidence, including one in the magnificent Musée de l'Arles Antique only a little further downstream from the site of the bridge.

It is museums such as this one which often create a more intimate picture of Roman cities and city life than the scattering of dry stones that is often all that remains. Monuments speak for themselves—theatres, triumphal arches, aqueducts—but daily life is made up of smaller, more fragile things. The Arles museum has assembled a great many of these domestic artefacts, and together they build up a sketch at least of what ordinary life was like in the new city which the Romans called Arelate. Pottery cooking- and serving-dishes retain the shine and freshness of vessels that look as if they were used and washed up only yesterday. Likewise bronze casseroles and frying-pans look their age only because of the patina of green they have acquired; and at least one elegant glass jug could have won an award at any exhibition of modern design in Europe or the United States today. With all these domestic utensils we are constantly aware of the indelible debt to Greece: just as Greek remained for so long the language of the Roman educated classes, so Greek household artefacts were the models which Roman domestic craftsmen chose to copy and to emulate. The noble shadow of Greek life and culture is never far away in the new Roman cities of the

New Cities... and How to Live

Province, whether in the form of kitchen pots and pans or floor mosaics illustrating scenes from Greek mythology—a special favourite (for reasons best left to the imagination) being that of Europa borne away naked by Jupiter/Zeus in the form of a bull.

Arles was not the first of the new Roman cities of the Province. The very first Roman settlement, Aquae Sextiae (Aix-en-Provence), was established as early as 123 BC; but virtually nothing of it survives. Then there is Narbo (Narbonne). This had been a colony since 118 BC, and later gave its name to the entire region of Roman southern Gaul, officially called Gallia Narbonensis. Like other new cities in the Province it became greatly expanded through veteran soldiers being given land here as a reward for their services, in this case the legion which had helped defeat Mark Antony and Cleopatra in the Battle of Actium. As a port (which it is no longer) Narbo came close to rivalling the Greek port of Massalia, while as a city it was described by the poet Martial as 'the most beautiful' in Roman Gaul. Again no more than a few fragments survive of the Roman city, though the local archaeological museum possesses one of the finest collections of Roman paintings to be found anywhere.

Nîmes, by contrast, still waves its Roman flag proudly. The two most conspicuous monuments, the amphitheatre and the perfectly preserved temple known as the Maison Carrée, feature in later chapters. Though the forum no longer survives next to the Maison Carrée, records of day-to-day life in this prosperous and pleasure-loving city are still there to be found. Nîmes was known to the Romans as Nemausus, the word deriving from a Celtic god of springs. Water, as always, was the key to where the Romans chose to build their settlements, and in no Roman city in the Province is the use of water—for domestic purposes, display, hygiene, health, and for luxurious self-indulgence—more in evidence than in Nîmes. It was the favourite city of the governor of the Province under Augustus, Marcus Agrippa, who personally sponsored some of its public buildings (though there is much dispute over precisely which ones); while a century-and-a-half later two even more generous benefactors were the Emperors Hadrian and Antoninus Pius, the latter being actually a son of the city, his mother having been born here.

By this time the citizens of Nîmes could enjoy the luxury of two sources of water; and these performed two distinct but complementary

ROMAN PROVENCE

Remains of a huge thermal complex at Cimiez, on the outskirts of modern-day Nice. Every town of any size in Roman Provence would have had an extensive area of public baths. Here at Cimiez there were separate baths for men and women.

functions in Roman city life. The colossal engineering feat of the aqueduct from Uzès by way of the Pont du Gard (described in Chapter 4) was the principal source of water for a variety of utilitarian purposes, from serving public buildings to providing an underground sewage system. It was this source of water which gave Nîmes the renown of being a city of fountains, which remains true to this day. It also provided one of the primary social venues of Roman city life—the public bath. Here was a focus not only for bathing and physical exercise but a place where citizens could read, play music, attend lectures or take advantage of that ultimate luxury of a winter day, the room equipped with the 'hypocaust' system of hot air rising from water heated beneath the floor. Altogether the Roman public baths performed the combined role of community centre, health spa and sports complex. They represent Roman life at its most egalitarian. Baths were available to all citizens except slaves, and accordingly they were cheap. For reasons of privacy rather than sexism separate baths were often provided for women, though there are accounts that on festive days mixed bathing was not uncommon, giving rise to inevitable charges of lewd behaviour by disapproving city fathers.

New Cities... and How to Live

Then there was the second source of water for the citizens of Nîmes. This was the famous spring dedicated to the Celtic god from whom the city took its name. And here, under the shadow of the city's defensive walls and the massive Tour Magne built by Augustus, the Romans transformed the spring they inherited into a sacred *nymphaeum* which formed the centre of a vast sanctuary, the spiritual heart of the new city. Today the sacred spring still flows abundantly, but in an elaborate environment of palisades and statuary which would have astonished—and perhaps delighted—the original Roman architects of the place. It has become the centre of one of the most elegant public gardens in France, created during the eighteenth century in a spirit of extravagant homage to its imperial past.

The importance of public baths in Roman Provence is hard to ignore. Like the aqueducts which fed them, they tend to have survived a great deal better than the normal disposable artefacts of Roman city life. Every town of any size in the Province would have had public baths of some kind, and the most sophisticated of these tend to date from the later centuries of Roman rule. One of the most striking is a huge thermal complex which was once part of the Roman town of Cemenelum—today Cimiez, the well-to-do suburb overlooking Nice and a wide spread of the Mediterranean. Nice, like so many coastal settlements at that time was a Greek town, Nikaïa; but the Romans wanted a military base and chose to establish it in a more strategic position in the foothills, taking over a former Gallic settlement. And in the first century AD the garrison town expanded into becoming the administrative capital of the entire Alpes Maritimes region, added to the Roman Province ever since Augustus Caesar had crushed forty-five Alpine tribes, and celebrated his success with the massive triumphal monument, the Trophée des Alpes (see Chapter 2).

The thermal baths of Cemenelum/Cimiez occupy an extensive area of what would have been the residential district of town. Built of small stones alternating with brick, the baths consist basically of separate rooms—hot, warm and cold—the hot room (*caldarium*) being heated by the usual hypocaust system, the floor supported on small brick pillars between which the hot air circulated. An added refinement at Cimiez was the provision of separate baths for men and women.

Today several touches of irony have been added unintentionally to

ROMAN PROVENCE

Part of the extensive Greek/Roman town of Glanum, near St.-Rémy: the foundation of one of the large private dwellings, known as the House of Atys.

Cimiez. Overlooking the excavated area of the baths stands a seventeenth-century Italianate villa which is now a museum devoted to a French artist who would have relished the sight of naked figures frolicking in the *caldarium*. He was Henri Matisse. But then, as a corrective, Cimiez also boasts a statue of a monarch who spent much time here in the nineteenth century, and who might have been rather less amused by such aquatic frolics: Queen Victoria.

※

Amid this wealth of surviving public buildings, noble monuments and astonishing engineering feats, the places where people actually lived day by day and night by night are among the hardest to find. Of all the records we have of Roman town and city life, ordinary houses are rarely more than shells, and our imagination has to do the rest. We generally know more about Roman drains than we do about Roman homes. There are important exceptions. At Glanum, tucked dramatically into the foothills of the Alpilles, the House of Atys is among several residences whose lay-

New Cities... and How to Live

out indicates a spacious and comfortable way of life, with refinements such as alcoves built into the walls to accommodate beds. At the top end of the scale there are lavish mansions of the wealthy such as the huge villa of Tauroentum complex (now a museum) along the coast east of Marseille at St.-Cyr-sur-Mer, which boasts magnificent mosaic floors and a pergola of stone columns over 260 feet in length commanding an unbroken view of the Mediterranean. Here was a cult of the Riviera at least a millennium-and-a-half before British royalty set the trend.

Vaison-la-Romaine: La Villasse and Puymin

The *villa* was always the country mansion: the town house was a *domus*, which none the less could be just as lavish. The most vivid record we have of Roman urban houses in the Province, and indeed city life in general, is in one of the smaller Roman cities in the northern area of modern Provence. This is Vaison-la-Romaine, two large areas of which have been uncovered so spectacularly that Vaison deserved to be considered the Pompeii of Provence. That so much of it has been rescued is due largely to the passion and commitment of one man, Canon Joseph Sautel, who supervised the excavations on the site from 1907 for almost fifty years.

The centre of the city, with its forum and public buildings, still lies buried under the modern town. But the two areas excavated reveal aspects of Roman city life which normally remain hidden. In one of these areas, La Villasse, a handsome paved street, raised and colonnaded, runs straight through this domestic district of the city in the manner of a modern high street, flanked by houses and shops, baths, gardens and fountains. Narrow by-streets and alleys branch off it, winding between the clustered buildings.

Nowhere in Provence does Roman city life feel as close and as real as in Vaison. You can almost smell the freshly-baked bread and the olive oil being squeezed from stone presses, and taste the rich desert wine of which Pliny wrote so complimentarily.

This was a very wealthy city, one of the most prosperous in the Province, and it is the houses which demonstrate it. They are spacious and grand, the largest covering an area of almost 55,000 square feet (as large as any house in Pompeii). This is the House of the Silver Bust, one of two prominent town-houses uncovered in the Villasse district. Its name is taken from the silver head of a man, presumably the owner who

A large *domus*, or town house in Vaison-la-Romaine, sometimes called the Pompeii of Provence.

was wealthy enough to have his portrait-bust cast in a precious metal, and which was found here. It is now displayed in the local museum, keeping company with three emperors, Claudius wearing a crown of oak, Domitian in armour, and Hadrian naked.

The *domus* was laid out in the approved high Roman style—a vestibule leading through to a partially-covered courtyard with rooms leading off it, among them a large dining-room for banquets; then to a colonnaded garden with a pool and fountain, and further rooms set around it including baths, latrines, store-rooms and servants' quarters.

The patricians of Vaison certainly lived in style. Impressive witnesses to their opulence are the enormous floor mosaics which all these town mansions possess. The most spectacular of these (now likewise in the museum) was lifted from the House of the Peacock in the second excavated area of Vaison, the Puymin district. The house takes its name from one of the finest mosaics in the whole of Roman Provence—a huge floor space with naturalistic details round the edges and in the centre a peacock in flamboyant display, a symbol no doubt of the proud owner himself. This is Roman art at its best: decorative and undemanding, a celebration of the good things of life. If wealthy Roman society was plagued by

New Cities… and How to Live

An indication of the wealth and splendour of a Roman town house: a massive floor mosaic from the House of the Peacock in Vaison-la-Romaine, now in the local museum.

terrors and doubts, we would never know it.

The last word on the strutting peacock world of Vaison should be left to that shrewd observer of Roman society, the architect and engineer Marcus Vitruvius, who would have been familiar with houses such as this one. He noted that 'private rooms are accessible only to invited guests. People of the lower classes have no need of a vestibule or a spacious atrium, as it is customary for them to pay their respects to others, and not for others to come to them.' Taken out of context these are words that might have been directed at Victorian England.

One other Roman city in the Province rivals Vaison in the richness of its private mansions. Vienne lies well to the north of modern Provence, in the Rhône Valley a shot distance to the south of Lyon. A former Celtic capital, Vienne became a vital base for Julius Caesar in the Gallic wars (as described in Chapter 2), and before long rose to be one of the richest of the new Roman cities, largely as a result of its command of the river trade north and south.

Not surprisingly the merchants of Vienne chose to live and work close to the river which was their livelihood. They needed space, both for

ROMAN PROVENCE

Gracious living: a microcosm of the natural world in a floor mosaic, from a private villa on the banks of the Rhône at St.-Romain-en-Gal.

storage and for their own luxurious mansions. Accordingly they had a stone bridge constructed across the Rhône (a remarkable engineering feat across such a broad and swirling river, of which sadly no traces remain); then they set about establishing a residential and industrial suburb on the western bank facing the city across the water. Today this is the expansive archaeological site of St.-Romain-en-Gal, transformed into an extended museum incorporating workshops, warehouses and—above all—mansions that were equal in splendour to those at Vaison. And, as at Vaison, it is the floor mosaics which are the most striking witnesses to this opulent society. Whereas in Vaison they graced the houses of city fathers and rich landowners, here they decorated the mansions of industrious merchants and river traders. Again the houses have been named after the mosaics found in them: the House of the Ocean Gods and the House of the Fire Mosaics. Round a central mythological theme each mosaic is also a delightful microcosm of the natural world: they are cameos of deer, ducks, horses, scenes of the hunt. Their wall paintings, too, reflect the same love of nature and of simple daily pleasures—gardens, flowers, grapes, fountains, wild birds.

New Cities... and How to Live

Always close by at St.-Romain, never out of sight, is the great green river, the Rhône, artery and lifeline of Roman Provence. Success and wealth lay predominantly in trade, as the vast riverside warehouses here bear witness. In the museum rests a full-size model of a cargo vessel of a kind that would have travelled the river carrying goods upstream to Lyon or downstream to Arles. The vessel is laden with wine barrels, a reminder that the wooden cask was an invention of Roman Gaul, where oak-trees were plentiful. The noble craft of barrelling wine was born here, and the wall-paintings and mosaics of the region demonstrate the enjoyment the Romans took from consuming it. A huge mosaic from a merchant's house in St.-Romain illustrates the legend of a Grecian ruler who was punished by the gods for outlawing the worship of Bacchus, the demented monarch killing his own son by mistaking him for a wine sack. Let that be a lesson, we feel the message to be. One of the few prohibitions known to rich Roman society was the denial of worldly pleasures.

Nîmes. Arles. Orange. Vaison-la-Romaine. Vienne. These are Roman cities long brought to light. Here the legacy of six centuries remains bright, and their monuments still dominate the modern town. But there are other Roman settlements in the Province which still lie buried in the undergrowth of centuries, waiting to be revealed. One of these is Ambrussum, in modern Languedoc midway between Nîmes and Montpellier. This was never one of the great Roman cities, more a well-fortified *oppidum* and service station at a key river-crossing on the road to Spain. In the lower town are the foundations of roadside inns for travellers, with a nearby forge, pottery, wells, bread ovens, a water-mill for grinding corn, even baths for weary travellers, in fact all the necessities for a small community reliant on passing trade.

Then, covering the entire hill above, lies the upper town, far larger but entirely invisible beneath a dense covering of scrub and evergreen oak. The only clue to the existence of a human settlement is a network of roads crisscrossing the hill, each paved with blocks of stone polished by two thousand years of traffic and weather, and deeply rutted by the wheels of carts which for so many centuries serviced the town. The roads lead eventually to open spaces where the town gates once stood, north and south; and between the gates, overlooking the valley and the far hills, runs a crescent of crumbling ramparts which cut a long swathe through the scrub—like a battered shell still protecting the invisible settlement.

Ambrussum is one of yesterday's Roman towns which very soon will become tomorrow's discovery. It will emerge from the undergrowth and astonish us. In several ways it exemplifies the control which the Romans maintained over this region, and why they succeeded for so long. Looking down from the hill of Ambrussum the eye falls on three images which symbolise that achievement and success. Firstly, the great road leading from Spain to Italy. Then the river it had to cross at this point. And finally what remains of the noble bridge that was built to carry it—about all of which there will be more to say in the chapter to follow.

The main street of a buried town: one of the stretches of Roman road in the unexcavated town of Ambrussum.

7.

Bridges... and the Oldest Road in France

The Romans laid a network of roads across the entire spread of their newly-conquered lands, until it became like a gigantic spider's web extending to every corner of the empire: 56,000 miles of road, it has been estimated.

All principal roads were meticulously levelled and then paved with stone blocks specially quarried from local stone, wherever that might happen to be. The initial purpose of such an elaborate network was purely military: it was the army that built the roads, and the army that first used them. Conquered lands needed to be kept under control and so legions needed to be moved speedily from one region to another, and when necessary to be recalled to Rome, or be reinforced from there. All roads did indeed lead to Rome, the empire's capital and ultimate command-post.

In the wake of the military came other users of the new roads, and who also played their part in keeping the empire in working order. For instance, with characteristic efficiency the Roman authorities instituted the Imperial Post, a creation generally attributed to that master-administrator Augustus Caesar towards the end of the first century BC. Messages could now be delivered to Rome by mounted couriers from any part of the empire, those from the Province likely to take less time than letters may take today. Towns being few and far between, in order to speed up the postal service a system of wayside inns was set up along the principal roads, one inn roughly every twenty miles. Each inn would have stabling and available horses which could be exchanged by travellers. Couriers engaged in the Imperial Post would therefore always have a choice of inns along the way; and in the case of highly important messages to the Roman Senate or the emperor himself an exchange of courier, as well as horses, might take place so that a rider could continue his mission through the night if necessary.

Following the course of the Rhône upstream, a section of the Via Agrippa, connecting Arles with Lyon.

Bridges... and the Oldest Road in France

The new roads soon proved to be of considerable economic as well as military value. They became trade routes. While rivers, particularly the Rhône, were the primary arteries for conveying goods of all kinds, from minerals to wine and oil, the roads provided key links to river ports such as Arles where produce could be loaded on to vessels heading upriver to Lyon or down the Fos canal to the Mediterranean and the flourishing port of Massalia. The roads attracted a continuous flow of travelling merchants and traders with their animals and loaded carts, and it was chiefly for their benefit that the inns were established at regular intervals along the way. Accompanying each inn there would often be further services for the wellbeing of travellers—a bakery, a cobbler, a saddler and in particular a blacksmith capable of shoeing horses. A roadside inn could become the heart of an entire miniature village; and invariably it would be situated close to a river or stream so that travellers' horses could be watered.

The Province was served by three such principal roads, and on a map they can be seen to form an inverted 'T', with three 'spokes' radiating outwards from Arles—east towards Italy and west towards Spain, while the central 'spoke' followed the River Rhône northwards towards Lyon and central Gaul.

The earliest of the three roads is the Via Domitia, named after the first Roman proconsul of the region, Domitius Ahenobarbus, who began the construction of it in 118 BC for the single purpose of providing military access to Spain where local tribes were proving less than contented at being subject to Roman rule. The Via Domitia has the distinction of being the first Roman road in France. In fact as the principal highway from Spain it long pre-dates the arrival of the Romans. It was the route which the Carthaginian general, Hannibal, took with his army and his elephants on his way to challenge the might of Rome in 215 BC. Many legendary centuries earlier still it was also the route Hercules is supposed to have taken as he headed back to Greece with his loot after completing the tenth of his twelve labours, the theft of the cattle of Geryon.

From Arles the Via Domitia headed north-east to what is now Haute Provence. But a more important road was created by Augustus, extending the line of the Via Domitia directly eastwards closer to the sea. This was the Via Aurelia, and it completed the vital military link between Spain and Italy. The Via Aurelia was literally 'the road to Rome'.

Finally there was the Via Agrippa, which followed the east bank of the Rhône northwards from Arles, and took its name from Augustus' most brilliant general, Marcus Agrippa, conqueror of Mark Antony and Queen Cleopatra at the Battle of Actium. Agrippa was also (according to the biographer Suetonius) a remarkable architect who according to tradition may even have been responsible for the Pont du Gard (see Chapter 4). Agrippa served two periods as governor of the Province under Augustus, and it would have been during his time in the region that he undertook another key task for his emperor: he travelled northwards along the road which was soon to bear his name, then at Lyon drew up a plan for the vast network of roads which Augustus was soon to build, radiating outwards from Lyon across the whole of Roman Gaul. Even if only half the achievements attributed to him were true, Marcus Agrippa must still stand as among the most gifted men Rome ever produced.

These, then, were the three principal Roman highways in the Province—east, west and north. Had there been a fourth they would together have formed the shape of a cross, with the city of Arles in the very centre. As it is, the fourth arm is a waterway, the famous Fos canal which Marius constructed at the outset of Roman occupation of the region, in order to bring supplies to his military camp while waiting for the vast army of the Teutones to cross the Rhône and challenge him.

Marius' canal has long been swallowed up by the shifting landscape of the delta. But roads are made of more durable materials—heavy cobbles set on a bed of gravel and edged with massive kerbstones and a ditch on either side. They were made to last, as sections of them at least have lasted. They survive as witnesses to so many centuries of travel; witness also to that Roman determination to impose the human will on the natural world, to be the master of that world, not its servant or its victim.

Old roads have an air of romance about them: their ancient stones carry echoes of journeys long ago, and none more so than the oldest road in

Bridges... and the Oldest Road in France

France, the Via Domitia. Along this great highway Roman legions marched to and from Italy and Spain, traversing the length of southern Gaul and in the process crossing two mountain ranges, the Pyrenees and the Maritime Alps. The road was a vital thread keeping a potentially rebellious outpost of the empire within the control of Rome. And as a vein running the entire length of this region it supplied the life-blood to what became the 'Province of Rome'.

Once north of the Pyrenees Domitius' highway cut straight across the plain of Roussillon towards the first administrative capital of the new Roman territory, Narbo. And in the open countryside the road he created is still there, more visible from the air than on the ground, slicing like a thin blade through the patchwork of modern orchards and vineyards. For the most part it is a mere track identifiable for what it is largely by that Roman insistence on making roads dead straight unless there happened to be a mountain in the way (even then the Romans had been known to move mountains).

In Narbonne itself a mere fragment of the paved road survives, but the town is bisected by a small canal, the Robine. Here one arch survives of a bridge over which the Via Domitia once passed, partly concealed ever since the Middle Ages by a tight cluster of dwellings that were built over it, somewhat in the manner of a rather more celebrated bridge, the Ponte Vecchio in Florence.

The next major river-crossing was at Baeterrae (Béziers); and whereas the genuine Roman bridge in Narbonne hides itself beneath houses, here in Béziers the handsome multi-arched bridge which has every appearance of being Roman is in fact mediaeval and later, though certainly erected on a Roman base. But then, one of countless accolades which history has bestowed upon Roman engineers is that their design of bridges remained the accepted standard for architects over the succeeding centuries virtually until the invention of the suspension bridge.

So many rivers and streams flow into the Mediterranean from the mountainous interior of Languedoc and Provence that for the engineers working on the Via Domitia it became a repeated test of their bridge-buildings skills. The next major bridge after Béziers was over the River Hérault. The area was low-lying and flat; hence the river was wide and prone to extensive flooding. In consequence the bridge of St.-Thibéry is believed to have been one of the longest of all the Roman

A crouching giant in midstream, the single remaining arch of the bridge at Ambrussum, which once carried the Via Domitia towards Nîmes.

bridges along the Via Domitia, though sadly only four of the original nine arches remain today—slender bands of stone stretching across the water.

The road continued eastward across the plain towards what is now Montpellier, its line wavering occasionally to circumvent a natural hazard: once again aerial photographs demonstrate how modern fields and vineyards have rarely obscured it, allowing the ancient road free passage, so to speak, across its former terrain. Beyond Montpellier, very soon there is yet another bridge, this time one of the most strategically-important in the entire region. This is the Pont Ambroix at Ambrussum. Once it straddled the fast-flowing and treacherous River Vidourle and the neighbouring water-meadows with no fewer than eleven stone arches, four of them across the river itself. Today only a single complete arch survives, yet its sheer bulk and rugged presence makes this one of the most dramatic sights in Roman Languedoc. It stands in mid-stream like a crouching giant.

The surviving arch is the central one, the largest and the strongest, rising 23 feet high and 32 across. When most of the other ten arches disappeared we have no idea, though it is likely that flood-water would

Bridges... and the Oldest Road in France

have played its part, and doubtless quite a few ancient farm-buildings in the area owe their masonry to those long-fallen arches. So much stone for free would have been hard to resist. In the river itself evidence of two further arches does survive, one on either side of the central arch. We know the bridge was still in use during the Middle Ages, a thousand years after it was built. Then there is silence. A seventeenth-century drawing by an artist from Nîmes shows a total of three arches. Then in the mid-1850s the celebrated artist (and revolutionary) Gustave Courbet made several visits to the area from Paris at the invitation of wealthy patrons, and during one of these visits he painted the Ambrussum bridge from the river-bank (a canvas now in the Musée Fabre, Montpellier). The painting indicates that by this time it possessed two arches, having lost the most southerly of the three at some stage since the seventeenth century. Finally, in September 1933 flood-water caused one of the last two arches to collapse. Since the 1980s the massive building stones from this most recent stage of disintegration have been hauled from the river and carefully stacked high on the bank. Yet enthusiastic plans to rebuild the fallen arch seem to have been shelved indefinitely and the solitary crouching giant seems destined to stand alone.

Dramatically powerful though it is, as we stand on that river-bank at the place where Courbet once set up his easel, the mind's eye longs to recreate the entire bridge as it once was early in the first century AD—all eleven arches stretched across the river and the adjacent fields to a length calculated to have been nearly 600 feet. That, had it still existed, would truly have ranked among the wonders of the Roman world.

So, how did they set about it, those Roman military engineers? There is no surviving record of the exact procedures they followed in constructing their bridges. None the less we know pretty well what took place. Limestone was their favoured material. Being a relatively soft stone it could be sawn relatively easily—in fact often more easily than timber which posed the problem of wood grain and knots. The art of cutting stone with a metal saw was nothing new: it had long been known, certainly to the Greeks, and even as far back as Ancient Egypt. The Roman architect and engineer Marcus Vitruvius, who was active about the time these bridges in the Province were being built, is as always a fountain of wisdom on Roman building methods. On how to cut stone he writes: 'When we have to build, let the stone be quarried two years before, not in winter but in summer, and let it lie and remain in exposed places.'

The arches themselves were supported by a wooden structure which held the weight of the stone blocks until each piece of the completed arch had been slotted into place and its weight distributed on to the piers on either side. Some bridges, such as the Pont du Gard aqueduct, were constructed with no mortar or binding material whatsoever (see Chapter 4), but even so mortar came to be widely used in Roman bridge-building. A method of mixing sand with lime (from burnt limestone) to produce a hardening substance was a practice the Romans inherited from the Greeks. But the most favoured mortar was *pozzolana*, made from molten volcanic ash, the name deriving from the town of Pozzuoli, north of Naples, where the crater of a dormant volcano spewed out quantities of hot mud and sulphurous fumes (as it still does to this day over an eerie 'lunar' landscape).

The arch was by no means a Roman invention as it was well known to Ancient Egypt as well as Mesopotamia. The Romans' contribution lay in vastly extending its usefulness to all manner of engineering projects, from civic buildings and thermal baths to bridges and aqueducts across rivers and ravines.

In all these applications the most pressing challenge to Roman engineers was always how to lift and manoeuvre immensely heavy blocks of stone once they had been cut and shaped in the quarries. Cut stone could be dragged more or less easily, or floated on barges; but once on site the blocks had to be hoisted, often above fast-flowing water, and set in place with the utmost precision or the arch would collapse. The engineers overcame these hazards by employing a combination of skills. Firstly they used tree-trunks as rollers to bring each block of stone to the position exactly below the arch-to-be. Then, by means of levers, wedges, winches, pulleys, wooden wheels, ropes and a healthy supply of manpower, the stone could be attached to a crane and gradually—with even more manpower—hoisted into place.

Great bridges like the one at Ambrussum and of course the Pont de Gard further to the north-east could never have been constructed, or even attempted, without exceptionally skilled engineers. But they

Bridges… and the Oldest Road in France

could also never have been built without a substantial labour force. One of the advantages of a standing army, which Marius had instituted in the very earliest days of the conquest of southern Gaul, was the existence of a pool of ready manpower whenever there were no wars to be fought. The army thus served a double purpose. And in doing so it attracted recruits with a useful variety of practical skills. The army became an esteemed and lucrative career for a Roman at all levels, from ambitious leaders and fortune-seekers to humble craftsmen: for the latter the pay was good, and at times of war the loot could be even better. What was more, for those serving in the Province the prospect of a retirement pension in the form of land was a further inducement. For a Roman soldier operating in conquered lands life could be pleasantly rewarding.

And then there were the slaves, who generally provided the bulk of the unskilled labour force, without even needing to be paid. It is fair to say that the massive engineering feats of the Romans, in the Province and elsewhere, might never have been achieved had this not been a slave society. Julius Caesar is said to have been responsible for more than a million slaves; while over the following centuries the slave population of Italy itself is believed to have risen to double that of its own citizens.

After Ambrussum the Via Domitia marched on to Nîmes before changing direction slightly and heading directly east across the plain towards the Rhône. And 'march' is the appropriate word. No other section of the great highway offers so repeated a reminder that this was primarily a military road: trade and private use came second. There are no spectacular monuments or bridges along this stretch, not even a stretch of ancient paving engraved with deep ruts like those we can still walk along at Ambrussum. Instead the route is often traceable only by milestones placed here and there by Roman engineers, each carved with the distance to the nearest town so that passing legions would know how far they had to march to the next place of rest. Each milestone also respectfully bears the name of the ruling emperor.

The shift of direction after Nîmes was for a sound practical reason: this was the need to select the most suitable place for an army to cross the Rhône. The river was notoriously unpredictable, prone to severe flooding, with a swift current and inclined to produce islands in mid-stream which were tempting stepping-stones but could disappear overnight. Hannibal had of course managed the crossing several centuries earlier with an army that famously included elephants; but it is doubtful whether the Roman generals were any more certain than we are today about where and how Hannibal had achieved it, and in any case the river was forever altering both its character and even its precise course.

There are three possible places where the Via Domitia may have crossed the Rhône – and maybe all three were used at different times. The first is at Beaucaire (Roman Ugernum), where it is probable that a wooden bridge once crossed by way of an island in mid-stream, both of which disappeared long before the Romans themselves departed. A second candidate is a mile or so further south, where it is believed there would have been a crossing by ferry or raft. Most likely of all is further south still, at Arles. Here we know that the Romans built a bridge of boats linking the town itself to the boatyards and warehouses across the river. The pontoon bridge would have had stone piers on either bank, and fragments of one of these are still visible. The bridge is sometimes described as the Pont de Constantin, though it is believed to have been built several centuries earlier at the time of Augustus. It is known to have survived in some form until the fourteenth century, the boats presumably having been replaced a great many times in the course of thirteen centuries. Yet the sole pictorial record of it we have is from a surviving Roman mosaic in Italy, at Ostia, the former port of Rome. Largely on the strength of this mosaic a realistic model has been made, on display in Arles in the Musée de l'Arles Antique, not far from where the original bridge of boats would have been.

Once on the east bank of the Rhône the great highway split into three. The Via Agrippa headed north, following the east bank of the river past Avignon, Orange, Valence and Vienne as far as Lyon, the gateway to central and northern Gaul. The road which continued directly eastwards, maintaining the long link between Spain and Italy, was now the Via Aurelia. As for the Via Domitia, from the same junction point near Arles it now took a route further inland across the centre of what is now Provence before veering north-east into the mountains,

Bridges… and the Oldest Road in France

following Alpine valleys as far as Italy, the Lombardy Plain and what today is Milan.

Continuing this journey from Arles the Via Domitia soon skirted the northern slopes of the Alpilles. One of the oldest cities in the Province—originally Celtic, then Greek, and ultimately Roman—lay out of sight a mile to the south in a fold of these jagged hills. This was Glanum (described in earlier chapters). But during the third century AD the place was sacked by Germanic tribes, and the inhabitants took the precaution of re-establishing themselves more securely right on the Via Domitia, the rebuilt settlement becoming what is now St.-Rémy.

For some distance after St.-Rémy evidence of the road's precise route becomes thin on the ground. We know that the next objective was the town of Cabellio, today Cavaillon, and in order to reach it the highway needed to cross the second-largest river in the region (after the Rhône): the Durance. If there was ever a bridge here at Cavaillon there is no record of it, and nothing remains. The Greek geographer Strabo mentions a ferry, but since he was writing several decades before the Emperor Augustus enlarged and developed the Via Domitia his evidence is inconclusive. The Durance was always a river of extremes, bringing torrents of floodwater down from the hills in one season, at other times so low that it could be forded. So, whether by bridge, ferry or ford, the road certainly entered Cavaillon, the sole surviving evidence being a small triumphal arch through which the Roman legions would have entered the town, except that to add to the general uncertainty the arch is not even where it originally stood (see Chapter 3).

The Pont Julien

If the bridge at Cavaillon remains a myth and a mystery nothing could be more startlingly real than the bridge which lies near the village of Bonnieux, roughly halfway between Cavaillon and the next Roman town, Apta Julia (today Apt). This is the Pont Julien, named after the ruling Roman family of Julius Caesar and, by adoption, of Augustus. Its three elegant arches carried the Via Domitia over another unpredictable river, the Coulon (or Calavon).

The impact of the Pont Julien is so powerful that we can find ourselves wondering whether the Romans really left at all, so effortlessly does it carry its great age. In fact for more than two thousand years the

ROMAN PROVENCE

Spanning the River Coulon in three long strides, the elegant Pont Julien. Two vents on either side of the central arch allowed for high levels of flood-water and melting snow from the high plateau.

bridge continued to be used by traffic of all kinds precisely as its builders originally intended—the only difference being that the first vehicles to cross it were Roman carts and chariots, whereas latterly they were cars and motor-bikes. It was a tribute to Roman engineering skills that not until the year 2005 did the needs of conservation finally cause the bridge to be closed to all traffic except bicycles and those on foot. A parallel bridge was constructed close by, a good deal less elegant than its historic neighbour but at least allowing passers-by to enjoy a clear view of one of the most handsome Roman structures in the whole of Provence.

The Pont Julien spans the river in three long strides. On either side of the central arch the two supporting piers possess a feature which speaks clearly on the nature of the terrain and in particular the temper of the River Coulon. This is a pair of arched vents, or large apertures, which perforate each pier, the purpose of which was to permit the flow of flood-water which might otherwise have put dangerous pressure on the piers and the arches between them. Standing on the rocky river-bed below on a soft summer morning it can seem hard to believe that such a limpid stream could possibly cascade through those tall vents fifteen feet above our heads. Then, by following the lazy meander of the river downstream among the giant boulders, we realise that its

Bridges… and the Oldest Road in France

The Pont Julien. Until recently cars could drive over it, but today only cyclists and pedestrians are permitted.

course has been carved over the centuries in a shallow ravine between banks that are precisely as high as those stone apertures in the bridge itself. This broad plain where the Via Domitia crosses the river over the Pont Julien lies between two high plateaux, the Luberon to the south and the Vaucluse to the north. The Coulon rises in the second of these, and is the principal channel down which rainwater and melting snow from the entire Vaucluse plateau is regularly conveyed on its way to the Durance further west, then to the Rhône and finally to the flooded Camargue and the sea.

The Pont Julien is an elegant witness to how well the Roman engineers knew their volatile river, and took the necessary steps to ride its temper.

A puzzling question remains: when exactly did they build it? The received wisdom gathered from many guidebooks is that the Pont Julien was constructed specially for the Via Domitia during the third century BC. Yet this confident verdict is deeply flawed, ignoring the fact that the Romans were not even in Provence at all until at least a hundred years later; also that Domitius Ahenobarbus only began the road which bears his name around the year 120 BC, during his spell as Rome's first proconsul in the region. The most likely date for the bridge is provided by a military milestone which was originally set up close to the bridge presumably to mark its completion and the opening up of the new road. The milestone is engraved with a much more probable date which, by the Christian calendar, would make the bridge completed just three years before the birth of Christ.

The dating of the bridge to 3 BC establishes the remarkable fact that this masterpiece of Roman engineering was used by traffic of all kinds continuously for a total of two thousand and eight years. And, assuming this date to be correct, the Pont Julien must belong to that period of consolidation and prosperity in the Province when Augustus, Rome's first emperor, was engaged in expanding and in places re-routing the Via Domitia. Old wooden bridges were coming down, being replaced by sophisticated structures like this one capable of withstanding the elements and—in some cases—the long passage of time.

After Apt the road continued north-east towards the southern foothills of the Alps. The next stage took travellers to the town of Segustero (Sisteron), hunched below its giant cliff. For some distance there are no traces of the road, and even its precise route is not entirely certain—until after the town of Forcalquier it begins to follow the left bank of that great trading river, the Durance. And here, near the village of Lurs, is the most secretive and least-known of Roman bridges in the Province—and furthermore one that is still in use. This is the Pont de Ganagobie, which crosses the wooded ravine of the River Buès at a point where it slices between two commanding hills. A modern parapet and metalled surface combine to disguise its antiquity to passing travellers: only by scrambling down to the stony river-bed and gazing up at the tall single arch, can we grasp that this was indeed a bridge constructed to carry one of the most important roads in Roman Provence.

Soon Domitius' historic highway begins to climb northwards into the Alps and beyond the reach of this book. Before it does so one further relic of the Via Domitia survives only a short distance from the little Ganagobie bridge. This is a place which by its very modesty brings to life the ordinary day-to-day business of travel in Roman Provence. It is simply a ford, a *gué*, built of hewn blocks of stone set close together, and crossing a stream called the Reculon.

The survival of spectacular engineering feats like the Ambrussum bridge and the Pont Julien can easily hide the fact that it was not only

Bridges... and the Oldest Road in France

major rivers which Roman roads needed to cross. In considerably greater numbers were the small rivulets and gullies, too shallow to merit a bridge, but which in rainy seasons could make the passage of a troop of soldiers or travelling merchants well-nigh impossible. Only carefully constructed fords wide enough for carts and chariots could enable a highway to function; and in a region where so many streams drained rain and snow-water from the mountains there would once have been hundreds of such fords. Yet the Gué du Reculon is said to be the only one to survive virtually intact along the entire length of the Via Domitia between the Pyrenees and the Alps. Built of thirty-four massive stone blocks, it is eighty feet in length.

Constructed on a diagonal in order to deflect the force of the current it was designed almost as a miniature dam; and so effective was it that it served as the principal crossing place for all traffic along this ancient road, which in post-Roman times became known as the 'route royale', until 1845 when an alternative road was opened—a length of public service only 160 years fewer than that enjoyed by the Pont Julien.

❧

Most of the surviving Roman bridges in the Province are those that served the Via Domitia, which is hardly surprising since no other Roman road in the region needed to cross quite so many rivers and ravines. Nor is it surprising that the road should also be the legendary route taken by Hercules while carrying out his celebrated 'labours': there may indeed have been times when the Roman engineers given the task of building the Via Domitia felt that they too were engaged in a labour of Hercules.

Of the other Roman roads in the region the Via Agrippa has no surviving bridges at all. Its route, following the east bank of the Rhône northwards from Arles, crossed few rivers of any size all the way to Lyon. The largest of these, and the most hazardous to cross, was the Durance, which flowed into the Rhône a little to the south of Avignon, though there are no records of how travellers would have crossed it. A short distance to the north of Avignon a smaller but even more volatile river had to be crossed. This was the Ouvèze, a virtually dry riverbed for much of each summer, yet prone to disastrous flooding after heavy rainfall in the hills. A modern parable illustrates the dangers besetting Roman travellers on the Via Agrippa as they made their way north towards Orange, Vienne and Lyon. In September 1992 the Ouvèze bursts its banks and caused catastrophic damage to the ancient town of Vaison-la-Romaine through which the river flows, as well as sweeping away a number of bridges in the area. The only bridge to survive the onslaught of floodwater was in the centre of Vaison itself, and it was a Roman bridge. Built in the first century AD, it still stands today, its single arch high above the generally placid river providing the main link between the upper and lower parts of the town.

The third of the major Roman highways in the Province, the Via Aurelia, was a continuation of the Via Domitia at the point when the latter veered off to the north-east towards the high Alps. From Arles eastwards the Via Aurelia completed the road link between Spain and Italy, and ultimately Rome itself. The journey along it from Arles to the Italian border takes in a number of important Roman sites along the coast, among them Hyères, Fréjus, Antibes, Nice-Cimiez and La Turbie; but surprisingly there is only one surviving Roman bridge along the entire length of it, and that is unspectacularly plain and hidden away among vegetation. This is the little Pont de Tuve, near the village of St.-Cézaire sur Siagne, ten miles from Grasse. It is no more than a simple stone hoop over a river in a tranquil rural setting, yet as a timeless image of travel it makes a poignant contrast to the Riviera and the frenetic motorway a short distance away.

Roman bridges could be discreetly functional, like the Ganagobie bridge and the Pont de Tuve. But they could also be displays of personal exhibitionism. If a wealthy citizen of Rome wished to be a benefactor, and at the same time be honoured by posterity for his generosity, what more suitable gift than to commission a piece of engineering of immense public benefit which also incorporated a flamboyant superstructure with the benefactor's name and instructions inscribed upon it, as though he were Caesar himself? Such a structure exists, not on the Via Aurelia itself, but on a secondary road which led from Arles to the flourishing port of Massalia. This striking piece of self-display is the Pont Flavien, a single span over the River Touloubre some thirty miles north-west of modern-day Marseille, but which is unique among Roman bridges in France for possessing a pair of ceremonial arches at

The single-span bridge at Vaison-la-Romaine, which has withstood the flood-waters of the River Ouvèze when modern bridges have collapsed.

ROMAN PROVENCE

A bridge flanked by two triumphal arches, the Pont Flavien carrying the Roman road between Arles and Marseille.

either end, embellished with four stone lions like crouching guardians, two at the top of each arch.

The name Flavien refers to a certain Caius Dominius Flavius; and an inscription on the bridge itself states that it was built under his instruction. Flavius describes himself as a priest of Rome. Why he should have donated a bridge, and why, since he came from Rome, he should have chosen to build it here, are leading questions to which we have no answer. We can only speculate from empirical evidence. As we approach this striking edifice, set in the midst of a bleak and unprepossessing landscape, it is obvious that this was intended to be a great deal more than a bridge: its single span over the river would have done the job without any grandiose superstructure. In practical terms the twin arches are entirely superfluous: they were intended simply to be arches proclaiming the glory of Rome, just as the four lions crowning them were intended to be emblems of Roman might and majesty.

It may be that a political motive lay behind the Roman priest's public-spiritedness. We know that the bridge was completed around

Bridges... and the Oldest Road in France

Symbol of Roman might and majesty crowning the bridge, one of the stone lions above the Pont Flavien.

the year 12 BC in the reign of Augustus Caesar. Only a few decades earlier his predecessor Julius Caesar had inflicted a crushing defeat on the Greek city of Massalia, stripping her of many powers and possessions as a reprisal for the city's support of Pompey in the Roman civil war (see Chapter 2). It would not be entirely surprising if a well-to-do Roman patriot, doubtless with connections in this region, should leave money in his will for a monument demonstrating to all users of the new highway connecting Roman Arles to Greek Marseille that they were doing so only by courtesy of the conqueror. It was a piece of pure architectural propaganda. Even a priest of Rome could enjoy pouring salt into old wounds.

In the entire Roman Empire there are reckoned to be 330 stone bridges for traffic which survive in some condition or other, as well as 545 aqueduct bridges. Those in Provence and Languedoc represent only a small proportion of these: yet they remain among the most eye-catching, and include, as we have seen, the Pont du Gard, probably the most famous of all Roman bridges anywhere.

There is a powerful case for regarding engineering as the most outstanding achievement of Roman civilisation. What is beyond question is that among those feats of engineering bridge building is second to none. One of the leading experts on Roman engineering, Professor Colin O'Connor, has even stated in his book *Roman Bridges*, that such bridge construction may be regarded as 'one of the most successful, extensive, and lasting of all human material achievements'.

8.
THE TEMPLES OF THEIR GODS

The Romans worshipped a great many gods. On the evidence of inscriptions, and monuments with specific dedications, the principal triad in the Province consisted of Jupiter, Juno and Minerva, all three borrowed from the mythology of Greece. Jupiter was the Greek Zeus, king of the gods; Juno was Hera, his consort; and Minerva was Athena, goddess of the arts. In addition the Roman pantheon included further deities adopted from Greece: Apollo, god of the sun, of wisdom and most of all of justice—hence the most revered and feared of all the Greek gods; Venus/Aphrodite, goddess of love and of beauty; Neptune/Poseidon, god of the sea; Diana/Artemis, goddess of wild animals, of hunting and of the moon; Mercury/Hermes, messenger of the gods and thence the god of commerce; and Mars the god of war.

Also from Greece came the cult of Bacchus/Dionysus, god of the crops and of wine; while from Egypt came Isis, from Anatolia Cybele and from Persia Mithras. Besides these, there were numerous local deities in southern Gaul whom the Romans took over from the various tribes they conquered.

In all, it perhaps resembled being ruled by a celestial government, each deity responsible for a particular department of human life, or a particular aspect of the natural world. The only truly home-grown gods the Romans worshipped were their own emperors, a succession of whom promoted their personal deification with unwavering dedication and self-aggrandisement.

The Romans constructed temples and shrines to one or other of these numerous gods everywhere they settled in the Province. The design of temples was taken from Greek monuments which they knew well, not only from mainland Greece but from the former Greek outposts in Sicily and, nearer home still, in the southern region of the Italian peninsula itself (in particular the temples of Paestum). Furthermore it seems often to have been Greek architects who designed and supervised the building of them. Today only relatively few survive, and with two outstanding exceptions (in Vienne and Nîmes), even those few exist only in fragments.

It is not hard to understand why this should be so. Temples generally suffered a good deal worse than other Roman monuments from the arrival of Christianity. Whereas roads, bridges and aqueducts, baths, theatres and even amphitheatres continued to have their uses in a Christian world, temples existed only to honour pagan gods and therefore needed to be destroyed by the new order—unless of course they could be converted into churches, as was sometimes the case.

The first Roman temple to be built in the Province has survived for that very reason, by being transformed in the Middle Ages into a church known as Notre-Dame-de Vie. The temple stands in the heart of the city of Vienne, in the Rhône Valley a little to the south of Lyon. It was a city which the Romans knew as Vienna (not to be confused with the modern Austrian capital of the same name). The temple was erected facing what was then the forum towards the end of the first century BC under the auspices of the Emperor Augustus, who as a self-appointed deity had it dedicated to himself. And in case there should be any doubt as to the identity of the deity Augustus had a statue of himself placed inside the temple. Half a century later the Emperor Claudius re-dedicated the building jointly to Augustus and Livia, who was Augustus' wife and Claudius' own grandmother. Roman deities were often kept in the family.

History has not generally been kind to Roman temples. Besides being torn down in large numbers by the Christian authorities in the fourth and fifth centuries, those that survived Christian zeal have inevitably suffered from comparisons with the noble Greek temples of which they were copies, however handsome they were in their own right—and the Vienne temple is certainly handsome, with its ranks of Corinthian columns on the façade and on either side. In more recent times they have suffered even more from the proliferation of banks, museums and opera houses all over the western world in which a classical façade became the universal symbol of pomp, probity and civic pride.

The Vienne temple has endured its share of transformations. After becoming a mediaeval church, with a solid wall constructed along each

The Temples of their Gods

The first temple built in Roman Provence, at Vienne, late first century BC, originally dedicated by the Emperor Augustus to himself.

side between the Corinthian columns, it was turned into a local meeting-place for the Jacobin Club in the wake of the French Revolution, and subsequently became a court of justice, a library and a museum—in that order. That it looks like a temple once again is largely due to the efforts of the nineteenth-century archaeologist, playwright and author of the novella *Carmen*, Prosper Mérimée. In his capacity as Chief Inspector of Historic Monuments Mérimée had the building comprehensively restored in the 1850s.

Searching for the legacy of the Romans can have the air of a treasure-hunt, and is often at its most rewarding when this is so. Ancient monuments which occupy the heart of a modern city soon become part of the urban landscape, stripped of their history: stage scenery. On the other hand those that need to be tracked down offer a special pleasure—a rare sense of having discovered something preserved alive in a lost world. One place that possesses this haunting quality in plenty is another temple, or a fragment of one, dating from the same period as the temple at Vienne. Midway between Salon and Aix-en-Provence, at

ROMAN PROVENCE

The remains of a former complex of temples in the grounds of a chateau near Vernègues, north of Salon-de-Provence, part of a holy sanctuary dating from the period of Augustus Caesar.

Vernègues, stands a sixteenth-century country mansion called Château-Bas. In the grounds of the chateau, amid the vineyards and scattered trees, rises a single fluted column twenty-three feet high and surmounted by a an elegant Corinthian capital. Next to it is part of a podium and a length of wall ending in a square pilaster engraved with a strange snake-like pattern writhing along the entire length of it. This is almost all that remains of a temple which once formed part of a holy sanctuary comprised of a whole group of temples and shrines dedicated to various Roman gods including Jupiter, Neptune, Mercury and Mars. We know little more, not even why this sanctuary was so important. Its echoes are too distant.

In the hilly country north-east of Aix, in what is now Haute-Provence, are the remains of another remote temple. The nearby town is Riez, on the edge of the Valensole plateau which in high summer turns blue with lavender as far as the eye can see. The Riez temple consists simply of four parallel Corinthian columns in an open landscape and visible from a great distance: the fate of many of the other columns

The Temples of their Gods

On the edge of the lavender-covered Valensole plateau, four surviving Corinthian columns of the temple at Riez, also built under the Emperor Augustus.

is to be found in the walls of the nearby Christian baptistery established in the sixth century. The temple was dedicated to Apollo and, like others in the Province, was built during the reign of the Emperor Augustus. Riez was originally an *oppidim*, or capital, of a Celtic tribe whom the Romans displaced to create their own settlement. Two centuries later retribution was enacted when other tribes descended on the place and destroyed it, leaving Apollo's temple in ruins, all but four of its columns scattered over the landscape for three further centuries until Christian monks arrived to make use of so much available building stone.

Nîmes: the Maison Carrée

There is one surviving Roman temple in the Province which stands alone for its remarkable state of preservation, and for its perfection of design and craftsmanship. This is the Maison Carrée in Nîmes. It is Roman civic architecture at its most sophisticated, deserving to be ranked in the same company as the Greek temples which inspired it. The only banal aspect of it is its name. *Carrée* means 'square', and 'the Square House' is the name

The Maison Carrée at Nîmes, the best-preserved temple in Roman Provence, believed to be the work of a Greek architect. Raised on a high podium overlooking the forum, it was built to dominate the city.

it has to live with—though in fact it is rectangular, like most classical temples, being almost twice as long as it is wide.

The raised entrance is through a portico supported by ten free-standing Corinthian columns. Ten further columns on either side are embedded in the wall of the inner sanctum, which was the shrine of the presiding deity. In more recent times this holy-of-holies held a statue of the god Apollo; though originally, under Augustus at the beginning of the first century AD, the temple was evidently part of the imperial cult. The early dedication on the façade of the building was torn away some time during the Middle Ages. Then in the eighteenth century a remarkable piece of detective work revealed its wording. A local scholar realised that by examining the holes in the stonework where the original bronze letters had been attached it would be possible to establish which letters were used to make up the inscription. He duly came up with a dedication whose translation reads 'To Caius Caesar, son of Augustus, consul, (and) to Lucius Caesar, son of Augustus, consul designate; to the princes of youth.'

The Temples of their Gods

The elegant Corinthian columns of the Maison Carrée. Its interior bears the marks of its subsequent uses—as a church, town hall, private house, stable, marketplace, storage-place for city archives, and finally a museum.

The rediscovered dedication tells several stories. Its date clearly has to be during the reign of Augustus (died 14 AD), who made the dedication to two young men described as his 'sons'. In fact Caius and Lucius were only his sons by adoption, chosen in order to perpetuate the dynasty (just as Augustus himself had been adopted as his heir by Julius Caesar). Their real father was Augustus' trusted friend and general, Marcus Agrippa, who had twice been governor of the Province and has often been credited with being the patron of the Maison Carrée. Undisclosed in the dedication is that the two 'princes of youth', Caius and Lucius, one or other of whom Augustus had hoped would succeed him, died before him. Whether they died after the dedication, or were already dead, we can only guess. In either case the Maison Carrée is a memorial to dashed hopes: and before long the imperial crown would be worn by a distant nephew of Augustus, Tiberius.

Such information, derived from the mere shadow of an inscription, adds a personal and poignant note to what in appearance is such a formal and public building. Like other Roman temples, the Maison Carrée was intended to dominate the city. It is raised high on a podium, and presided loftily over the public forum, which in recent times has been clear of buildings and general clutter to give the temple the commanding site it originally occupied. The forum was the citizens' gathering-place, and the main function of the raised podium was to provide a platform from which public announcements could be made, or religious and civic ceremonies conducted. Fifteen stone steps led from the forum up to the podium, the idiosyncratic view being that the uneven number was chosen deliberately so that the visitor would always reach the platform on the same foot as the one he started with—the significance of which has been eroded by the passage of time.

We almost never know the names of Roman architects or artists, but details of the design and decoration of the Maison Carrée have suggested that the man responsible for the great Nîmes temple was a Greek. Visible from below (with some difficulty) is a magnificent frieze extending right round the building, carved with a delightful ornamental motif of roses and acanthus leaves. For those with even sharper eyes it is claimed that the line of Corinthian columns along the length of the temple has been given a slight convex curve: this was an architectural subtlety known as *entasis*, invented by the Greeks and applied most notably to the Parthenon in Athens, its purpose being to correct the optical illusion that a straight line of columns may appear to bulge.

The Maison Carrée's survival, in almost unscathed condition, is a tribute to the gods of fortune. With the arrival of Christianity in the fourth century, like the temple in Vienne it became a church. Once more suitable places of worship were built in Nîmes it became the local town hall, acting as a convenient meeting-place for the city's bigwigs. Then, in the sixteenth century it became what must have been an extremely uncomfortable private house occupied by one of the cathedral canons. Before long it was deemed more suitable for horses than human beings, and remained a stable throughout the French Revolution, some of its pillars being narrowed to allow the passage of hay-carts. There followed a period when it served as a public marketplace, then as a storage-area for the city's archives. Finally in 1823 it became a museum, housing classical and other works of art until the opening of the present archaeological museum nearby. The ceiling, designed in the Roman style, dates from that period.

The Temples of their Gods

And it is here, formerly in the Maison Carrée, where the most celebrated Roman statue to be found in the city is displayed. This is the Venus of Nîmes. Once again, as in the temple itself, the creative hand of Greece is invisibly present in the delicacy and elegance of the carving. The Romans worshipped their goddess of love as fervently as they did any other deity: witness the number of Roman statues of Venus which have survived. Mostly these seem to have been private commissions, as the Venus of Nîmes almost certainly was. Whatever her origin, she suffered the fate of other pagan deities. She was discovered in the late nineteenth century during building works in the city, smashed in pieces. Today she remains a serene tribute to the restorer's art.

A final word on the Maison Carrée. Having been a hostage to fate for almost two millennia, at the time of writing the great temple now suffers the further trial of being hidden under wraps for extensive renovations. As a result the eye becomes focused on its striking new neighbour, the glistening glass Carré d'Art, designed for displays of contemporary art by the British architect Norman Foster, and incorporating in a post-modernist idiom some of the principal architectural features of the Maison Carrée itself. Needless to say, local traditionalists have had their feathers ruffled by Foster's imaginative tribute to his Roman forebears. Welcomed or not, the Carré d'Art has given Nîmes a startling glimpse of the twenty-first century.

As with so many Roman towns in the Province, the origin of Nîmes/Nemausus lay in a Celtic shrine which the Romans adopted as their own, and proceeded to expand into one of the most important sacred places of worship and pilgrimage in the region. The very word Nemausus was taken from the name given by the Celts to the god of the local spring (see Chapter 6). The Celts venerated natural sources of water: these were seen as the holiest of sanctuaries, and they were presided over by a deity, or spirit, often possessing oracular and healing powers. The name of the god invariably became that of the settlement which grew up round the sacred spring.

The Romans shared the Celts' veneration of such places and 'Latinised' the names of the various deities: often this is the only clue we have of what their gods were called, there being no written Celtic language. Early in the first century AD the philosopher and dramatist Seneca declared that wherever there was a natural spring people should erect an altar and make ritual sacrifices. These sanctuaries were sometimes known as *nymphaea,* suggesting that—at least in common practice—these sacred springs had more sensuous associations, being seen as the habitat of water nymphs rather than of a single stern deity. *Nymphaea* were generally stone basins set around the sacred spring. Here people would gather to fetch water for sacred rituals; besides which a sanctuary might also serve as a focus of solemn public ceremonies, even weddings.

A number of such *nymphaea* have been located in the Province, some of which, like Roman temples, later became Christianised. The sense of a magic presence aroused by natural springs, of something indefinably sacred, was felt as strongly by early Christians as it was by the Celts and Romans: hence so many of the holiest Catholic shrines throughout Europe have been established on the site of springs or wells that had been venerated centuries before the Christian era. One of the most haunting sanctuaries in the Province lies not far from the Rhône near Montélimar. The Valley of the Nymphs, as it is known, lies in a cleft of the hills a mile from the village of La Garde-Adhémar. The sacred spring bubbles out of the hillside into a long stone basin sheltered by tall oaks and lime trees and accompanied by a chorus of bird-song resounding across the valley. A stone altar was found here inscribed with a dedication to the water-nymphs. A tiny early-Christian chapel stands by the side of the water—a token of the continuity of faith in the spiritual power of springs from one religion to another, Celt to Roman to Christian. The valley itself is a serene and evocative place: it requires only a slight stretch of the imagination to see fleeting images of nymphs in every shadow and reflection in the water. Here would be a perfect setting for *A Midsummer Night's Dream:* Oberon and Titania, king and queen of the fairies, would feel this to be their true realm.

More celebrated among sanctuaries to the gods of water is the Valley of the Sacred Spring at Glanum, that Celtic/Greek/Roman town wedged among the dramatic hills of the Alpilles to the east of Arles, and a place which is seminal to so much of the early history of Roman Provence.

It is another haunting place. The name Glanum derives from that of the Celtic god Glanis. And from the very beginning the settlement appears to have grown up and flourished round a spring which was held to be sacred and to possess healing powers. The Romans inherited its fame, and further enriched the city until it was destroyed under their very eyes by invading tribes in the third century AD, after which Glanum vanished without trace for seventeen hundred years until rediscovered and laid bare early in the twentieth century.

In this most evocative of ancient sites in Provence the Sacred Way threads its way through the shell of the Celtic, Greek and Roman city, the mountains on either side hanging closer and closer as the valley narrows. On the right a broken flight of stone steps stumbles upwards towards the bare cliff-face to what was once a rock sanctuary. Across the Sacred Way opposite the steps a passageway leads down to the underground spring which flowed into a long stone basin, walled in and still retaining one of the arches that once enclosed the shrine. Here was Glanum's inner sanctum, where for centuries people trudged in their thousands to pray and be healed. An altar was found during excavations dedicated to the god who gave his name to the city, Glanis. The deity was Celtic, yet the inscription is in Latin: yet another mark of the Romans' ability to make inherited gods their own. Likewise, the names of at least ten other healing deities are inscribed here: and besides that of the Celtic healing god Belenos are the names of Mercury, Apollo and—more surprisingly—Hercules. Largely on account of his legendary journey across this region in the course of carrying out his twelve labours, the name of the most famous of all Greek heroes, altered from Heracles to Hercules, became added to the list of deities honoured here, becoming worshipped as a guardian of the holy spring of Glanum. And so the mythology of the Celts, Greeks and Romans continued to blend, melting into a shared faith in the sacred and life-giving powers of natural springs

Had the city of Glanum survived, then its sacred spring and sanctuary might well have become as popular an urban landmark as its counterpart in Nîmes. But here the reverse of destruction took place. Not only did Nîmes become among the most prosperous of Roman cities in the Province but the shrine to the god Nemausus expanded into one of the most elegant pleasure gardens in Europe, forming the

The Temple of Diana, Nîmes, a mysterious Gallo-Roman religious site.

focus of the public park known today as the Jardins de la Fontaine. At the time of the emperor Augustus pilgrims flocked here, just as they did at Glanum, supplementing their prayers to the god with coins tossed into the sacred waters, much as tourists do today in Rome's Trevi Fountain, so perpetuating a long-standing tradition of appealing to the water gods with a little cash.

Eighteenth-century landscaping has largely obliterated what must once have been a greatly extended sanctuary covering much of the area below Augustus' Tour Magne. One curious building remains, or at least part of it remains. This is the so-called Temple of Diana, dating from the second century AD. It is an impressive wreck of a building. Tradition relates it to Diana in her role as goddess of the moon, for which there is no substantial evidence at all. It is not even known what this so-called temple was built for: learned opinion has variously claimed it to have been a shrine to some unidentified deity, part of a large complex of Roman baths and even a library. In the ninth century it became an early Benedictine convent. When Nîmes became a predominantly Protestant city it was abandoned. The subsequent wars of religion did it no favours, and the Catholics finally wrecked it to prevent Protestant troops using it as barracks. Two centuries later much of what had survived became convenient building-stone for the present Jardins de la Fontaine. With such a tormented history it is surprising that anything of Diana's temple remains at all. It is, in the end, an intriguing architectural puzzle.

The Temples of their Gods

The Romans adopted a pragmatic attitude to death: you died, and that was that. For practical and hygienic reasons you were buried outside the city walls in a necropolis established by the roadside. Passers-by could pay their respects, and you would never be entirely forgotten. It was all very unlike the way of the Christians who followed, with their preoccupation with the afterlife and the judgmental punishments that inevitably accompanied it. The Romans were less interested in their sinners than in their heroes. And like so much else that they borrowed from the Greeks they adopted the belief that the brave and virtuous found a final resting-place in the *Elisii Campi*, the Elysian Fields.

Elysian Fields was the name given to the most celebrated necropolis in Roman Provence, known now in its abbreviated French version as Les Alyscamps, in Arles. In recent times its fame has been increased by two impoverished artists both of whom were drawn to the place and set up their easels here: Gauguin and Van Gogh. Yet Les Alyscamps was always a special place. Established just outside the walls of the city beyond the Porte d'Auguste, it flanked the new road heading eastwards towards Italy, the Via Aurelia. This meant that anyone approaching Arles from that direction would need to pass between this double line of tombs and monuments before entering the city. The Romans were proud of their dead, and proud to display their tributes to them as if they were a guard of honour.

So great was the fame of Les Alyscamps that bodies were transported here for burial from all over the Province, hugely expanding the size of the place. Its prestige was even further enhanced when Arles became one of the earliest cities in the region to be Christianised: Constantine I, the first Christian emperor, regarded Arles as his favourite city after Rome itself. The transformation of Les Alyscamps into a Christian cemetery was facilitated by one of those convoluted legends born of hope and dreams upon which so much early church history rests: this was the belief that among those who lay buried here was a certain Trophimus who had been sent from Rome during the third century at the time of persecution to spread the gospel, and had become the first bishop of Arles. Further colouring of this legend was added in the fifth century when it was reported that that Christ himself had appeared at the bishop's burial. And so Trophimus became St. Trophime, later to give his name to one of the most beautiful churches in the region, Arles'

ROMAN PROVENCE

Les Alyscamps, the celebrated burial-ground in Arles. Its majestic avenue of Roman tombs became Christianised, dominated by the handsome bell-tower of St. Honorat's church.

twelfth-century former cathedral, whose magnificent carved portico mirrors the shape of so many triumphal arches of Roman Provence.

The blending of faiths and cultures is a recurring feature of Roman Provence: Celtic, Greek, Roman, Christian—whether in places, mythologies or deities there is a continual handing-on of stories and beliefs, a dressing-up of borrowed material which suggests a kind of universality transcending the conflicts that so often tore them apart. Who can tell what that binding force was? Yet somehow Les Alyscamps typifies it. The Celtic and the Greco-Roman gods become banished. The great avenue of Roman tombs and monuments is now presided over by the proud bell-tower of St. Honorat's church. Christianity has won. Yet without that majestic corridor paying homage to the Roman dead this place would be just another leafy park with a lofty church nearby. Lawrence Durrell, in his delightfully-meandering tribute to Provence, *Caesar's Vast Ghost*, describes Les Alyscamps as 'the most poetic corner of Arles', adding that although the Christian and pagan burial grounds were once separated 'the area has gradually contracted as the centuries passed.'

No wonder Gauguin and Van Gogh, so violently opposite in temperament and outlook, should have found common ground and a rare peace here in this serene avenue where Romans and Christians lie side by side.

9.
THEATRES AND AMPHITHEATRES

Provence has the best-preserved Roman theatre of any throughout the empire: this is in Orange, now regularly used for operatic performances that are a good deal more sophisticated than many of the shows which would have been staged here at the time of the Emperor Augustus when this theatre was constructed.

Roman theatre, like so much else in the Roman world, evolved largely from the culture of Athenian Greece. Apart from the surviving plays of Terence and Plautus (second and third centuries BC) we know little about the earliest Roman stage-plays except that they were generally comedies, loosely in the tradition of the Greek playwright Aristophanes, and often somewhat bawdy, a tradition which seems to have persisted well into the imperial era. The Emperor Augustus is reported by his biographer Suetonius to have felt the need to keep a strict check on the licentious behaviour of actors on stage.

Successive Roman emperors understood that the theatre could become a vehicle for more powerful material than lewd entertainment. Plays began to be composed on heroic themes which were thinly disguised exercises in propaganda promoting the imperial cult. The principal dramatist in this vein was Seneca, also a statesman and philosopher, whose plays found huge favour among the Roman ruling classes at just the time when the new stone-built theatres at Orange and elsewhere in the region were replacing the temporary wooden structures in which plays had previously been performed.

Seneca's dramas leant heavily on the classical Greek tragedians Aeschylus, Sophocles and Euripides, with appropriate Greek heroes such as Agamemnon, Oedipus and Heracles. But whereas the heart of Greek tragedy—and its greatness—lay in the fateful struggle between humankind and the dark forces of destiny, Seneca's dramas had no such soul-searching ambitions. Majestic splendour coupled with blood-curdling melodrama was more the order of the day. Tender studies of

Symbol of imperial grandeur, the double-life-size statue of the Emperor Augustus acknowledging the adoration of the audience in the great Roman theatre at Orange.

vulnerable humanity grappling with fate were not for Seneca, and certainly not for Augustus and the emperors who immediately succeeded him, Tiberius, Caligula, Claudius and Nero. Subtleties of human nature were left behind.

This cult of imperial grandeur is reflected in the architecture of the theatres themselves. Where the Greeks made use of a stage wall as a necessary background to the action as well as for acoustical reasons, the Romans raised the wall to a massive three storeys, as high as the topmost tier of seats in the auditorium beyond. Furthermore the wall itself was constructed with numerous niches, or alcoves, designed to display statues of appropriate gods: and, as the theatre in Orange makes clear, the largest alcove was reserved for a statue of the most appropriate god of all in the eyes of the ruling emperor—namely himself. The marble stature of Augustus at Orange, more than twice life-size, stands in the very centre of the stage wall, the emperor's left hand raised in condescending acknowledgment of the applause of nine thousand worshipping spectators in the semi-circle of seats facing him.

Where possible the bank of tiered seats, known as the *cavea*, was cut into a convenient hillside. Then, completing this spectators' area, above the highest tier of seats, ran a semi-circle of stone columns forming an elegant colonnade which originally supported a protruding roof to provide some protection for those seated below. At the base of the tiers the small semi-circle between the stone seats and the stage was known as the *orchestra*, and was where special chairs would be placed for the benefit of high-ranking officials and distinguished guests. The stage itself was slightly raised, ensuring that the view of spectators in the front tiers was not entirely obscured by the high and the mighty. The floor of the stage was laid in marble, some of it in mosaic, with various concealed hatches which enabled stage-hands to perform all manner of tricks, with objects appearing from apparently nowhere, or disappearing likewise. Plays were only part of the entertainment on offer. Jugglers, acrobats, magicians and mime artists were among regular attractions.

In all, Roman theatre seems to have been a rich mixture of melodrama and circus, of heroics and conjuring-tricks.

The largest surviving theatre in the Province—indeed one of the largest in the entire Roman world—is in Vienne, on the east bank of the

ROMAN PROVENCE

The theatre at Vienne, the largest in Roman Provence. Its tiers of seats, set into the hillside, were excavated only a century ago and are now the scene of a popular summer jazz festival.

Rhône a short distance to the south of Lyon. As with the theatre in Orange its rising tiers of seating were set into a convenient hillside, known today as Mont Pipet. And from here, on either side of the stage wall, Roman theatregoers would have been able to enjoy striking views of the great river meandering southwards, with its expanse of shipyards and warehouses along the far shore. In fact people are likely to have been able to see over the top of the stage wall itself since there were no fewer than forty-six tiers of seats designed to accommodate more than 13,000 spectators.

The Vienne theatre appears to have remained constantly in use well into the Christian era and the reign of Constantine: then, in common with so many Roman public buildings it fell into disuse with the collapse of the empire and literally disappeared, finally to be unearthed in the 1920s and to become the venue in recent years of a popular summer jazz festival—which one likes to think the Romans would have applauded, perhaps more warmly than they did a giant statue of their emperor-god.

Theatres and Amphitheatres

Another theatre from the Augustan era is in the very centre of Arles, the heartland of Roman Provence. It is smaller and more intimate in scale than the theatre at Vienne, with thirty-three tiers of stone seating which could accommodate around 10,000 spectators. Of the original stage wall only two columns survive, standing in romantic isolation—Henry James once described them as 'like a pair of silent actors'. Archaeologists have revealed a tantalising fact about these two columns: the marble of one of them was apparently quarried in Italy, at Carrara, while the second one came from a quarry in North Africa. Who knows why? Apart from offering a glimpse of Roman mercantile enterprise, we draw a blank. The zealous new Christians who began to build churches in Arles from the fifth century are largely responsible for the disappearance of the stage wall: here was building material readily on hand.

In time the churches disappeared. But by the seventeenth century there was a Catholic convent on the site; and when a new water system was being dug for the inmates builders came across a fine marble statue of Venus buried among the ruins of the theatre. Not being exactly suitable for a convent the Venus of Arles is now displayed in the Roman rooms of the Louvre in Paris. A more grandiose discovery on the same site was a larger-than-life torso of the Emperor Augustus which would once have gazed out at the spectators in Arles much at its clone had done in Orange. In the absence of a stage wall, the imperial torso now graces the Musée de l'Arles Antique, a short distance away near the river.

The smallest of the surviving theatres in the Province forms part of the excavated Roman city of Vasio, now Vaison-la-Romaine, the 'Pompeii of Provence' set in the lee of the region's highest mountain, Mont Ventoux, whose plentiful springs supplied the city with all the water it could possibly need, irrigating its orchards and fields and contributing to the comfort and wealth for which the place was renowned. Vaison was always a rich city, though relatively small; its theatre could hold 6,000 spectators in thirty-two tiers. And crowning the highest tier is a semi-circle of marble pillars, the elegant remains of the colonnade which all Roman theatres once had, and of which—with the exception of fragments—this is the only surviving example in the Province.

Maybe it was on account of Vaison's affluence that the original theatre, dating from the time of Augustus, was rebuilt a little over a century later during the reign of the Emperor Hadrian—an event which seems to have been marked in spectacular fashion by a statue of the emperor stark naked, later found on the site and now on prominent display in the small local museum.

Orange: the Theatre

In sheer prominence there are few monuments in Roman Provence and Languedoc which can match the theatre in Orange. It looms massively in the centre of the old town, its craggy bulk quite out of proportion to the neighbouring houses. It seems to inhabit a different world created by a race of giants. Its weathered walls of dark stone rise a hundred feet above the streets, its long array of arches like so many sunken eyes gazing down at us small people down below.

Orange is unique in the region for having retained its stage-wall, and from outside the theatre this dominates the whole area like a gigantic cliff-face you would not want to climb. Behind this vast wall the open stage faces a sloping auditorium which is gouged out of the hillside in a familiar semi-circle of stone tiers, designed to seat 9,000 spectators. This makes it marginally smaller than the theatre at Vienne, though appreciably larger than that at Vaison and approximately the same size as the one at Arles, though the latter would have looked equally imposing had the early Christian fathers not recycled its stage wall for church-building.

As it is, Orange has no equal among surviving Roman theatres anywhere. Its site helps—the fact that the semi-circle of seating was carved into a natural hillside, and the stone from the hill could be used for the seating itself. Inevitably much of its former splendour has gone. Originally the theatre bristled with stone columns, possibly more than a hundred of them set up around the auditorium, of which a mere six now stand, re-erected during major restorations during the 1920s. The massive wall behind the stage was once faced with marble, and inset with numerous carved figures of gods and goddesses placed in the various niches; and these formed a permanent background of presiding deities to the bloodcurdling melodramas regularly performed there. The only one of these statues to have survived is the central figure of the deified Emperor Augustus, and this was pieced together from fragments retrieved from heaps of rubble during the 1930s—first a leg and the torso, and later his

The Orange theatre today, unique in still possessing its original stage-wall along with its presiding statue of the Emperor Augustus. As usual the auditorium, designed to seat 9000 spectators, was cut into the hillside in a semi-circle. Its perfect acoustics have made it an ideal venue for concerts and celebrated operatic productions.

ROMAN PROVENCE

The Orange theatre as it looked early in the process of restoration in 1898.

head and the arm raised in imperious salute to an adoring crowd. Also found on the site were the broken remains of a statue of Venus, goddess of love, a deity rarely absent from any Roman scene of entertainment or worship. Her statue would have occupied one of the niches in the great wall, while the emperor's own larger-than-life statue was set, as it is today, right above what was known as the royal door, one of three entrances in the wall through which actors made their entrance on to the stage.

As with so many historic sites in France the present state of the Orange theatre owes a great deal to the vision of Prosper Mérimée. It was during his period as Chief Inspector of Historic Monuments in the mid-nineteenth century that the first serious study and restoration programme was begun here. By 1898 significant renovation had taken place, but great chunks of masonry still littered the site and many rows of seats had not yet been replaced. The major work on the theatre was conducted much later, during the 1920s onwards, by the distinguished French archaeologist, Jules Formigé, who worked on so many monuments in this region including another Roman theatre in far worse condition, at Arles. Mercifully, at Orange enough had survived for Formigé to re-create a setting now universally welcomed as one of the finest venues for open-air operatic performances in the world.

The theatre at Orange is a reminder that so many of the great building enterprises of the age of Augustus were constructed to satisfy a taste for public entertainment. It is impossible not to feel this to have been an era when spirituality was put on hold. Before long the Christians were to change all that.

※

The Romans owed their theatre to the Greeks—both the concept of it and its basic architecture. But the appeal of dramatic events taking place on an open stage before a massed audience soon opened up exciting further possibilities. In Greek drama all violent action took place off-stage, conveyed to the audience by reported speech. Not content with such theatrical decorum the Romans found a way of presenting violence centre-stage before people's very eyes. They took the traditional semi-circle of the auditorium and made it a complete circle, with the tiers of stone seats now totally surrounding the scene of action. The action itself was that sport so beloved of romantic novelists and Hollywood film directors, gladiatorial combat; and the new arena in which it took place was that blood-stained witness to the Romans' appetite for cruelty dressed up as sport: the amphitheatre.

If there were to be a single image representing the civilisation of Ancient Rome it would surely have to be the amphitheatre, the most dominant and eye-catching of all Roman buildings. Here was public entertainment at its most popular, and to which everyone except slaves would have gone, though women (at the insistence of Augustus) were required to sit on the higher terraces so as to be at a suitable distance from the blood and savagery. Local Gauls, who often made up the majority of a town's population, would certainly have been included, especially those town-dwellers who had become converted to Roman life and pleasures.

The largest and most famous amphitheatre is of course the Coliseum in Rome, completed in 83 AD and in its heyday capable of seating 50,000 spectators. There had been a predecessor a century earlier which lasted some seventy years until it was destroyed by fire at the time of Nero. Earlier still the then-flourishing city of Pompeii had boasted the very first stone amphitheatre, completed about the year 70 BC.

Before this time, as we know from the Roman historian Livy, the gladiatorial sports associated with the amphitheatre had been practised for many centuries either in the open forum—the public meeting-place—or in temporary wooden structures. So, by the time the Romans conquered and settled in Provence and Languedoc there already existed a long tradition of such sports. On the other hand it appears that they only achieved the status of the empire's most popular entertainment once they became patronised by the emperors themselves, who made extravagant use of them to further the cult of imperial glory. Pliny the Elder, writing in the third quarter of the first century AD, asserted that gladiatorial combats had by now reached the remotest towns.

Only a minority of these events would have taken place in stone-built arenas, and these would have been in the larger towns. A small number survive in Provence and the Riviera—the wreckage of an amphitheatre in Nice-Cimiez, and a small but more complete example in Fréjus, both of them on the Mediterranean coast. But the two outstanding amphitheatres surviving in the region, both built within a hundred years of the establishment of imperial rule, are those in Arles and Nîmes.

Disagreement among experts over the respective dates of these remarkable monuments has long been in full swing. Weighing up the different verdicts it seems most likely that both arenas were completed late in the first century AD, at about the time that Pliny was writing about the expanding popularity of gladiatorial sports. The Nîmes amphitheatre is probably the earlier of the two, and is in some respects a miniature version of the Rome Coliseum completed at much the same time. It is also the best-preserved amphitheatre anywhere in the Roman Empire. Capable of seating at least 20,000, its spectators could be protected from sun and rain by giant awnings held up by poles projecting from deep sockets in the upper stonework, still clearly visible.

Like all major engineering projects which the Romans undertook the Nîmes arena was meticulously thought-out and planned according to tried-and-tested principles. In this case the rules had been laid down by that architectural genius and master of common sense nearly a

Theatres and Amphitheatres

The amphitheatre at Arles, capable of seating more than 20,000 spectators, and showing two of the mediaeval towers erected above the outer wall when the theatre was used as a fortress. Today it is used regularly for bull-fights.

century earlier, Marcus Vitruvius. In his classic work, *De Architectura*, Vitruvius insisted that 'there should be sufficient gangways for those making their way up not to have to cross those going down.' Accordingly the Nîmes architect made the simple calculation, which could so easily have been overlooked, that the lower staircases carrying double the human traffic should be made considerably wider than those higher up. As so often in practical matters the Romans got it absolutely right.

The amphitheatre in Arles is marginally bigger than its Nîmes sibling, but wears a more battered look. Again it was capable of seating rather more than 20,000 spectators. A somewhat eccentric calculation has been made, that hardly a single one of the sixty exterior arches is of the same height or width as its neighbour. A more obvious difference in appearance is the presence of three lumpen square towers protruding above the rim of the building. There used to be four of these, and they were added in the twelfth century when the amphitheatre was transformed into a fortress—and not just a fortress, but a town too. Within the circular walls an entire settlement was created composed of several hundred houses and at least one church, supporting around 1500 inhabitants—all of whom doubtless contributed to the battered look of the place. Once again it was not until the period of Mérimée and the nineteenth-century romantic urge to restore the past that the mediaeval slum township was cleared away, and the arena returned to its original role as a venue for bloodthirsty sports.

One small detail is indicative of the use to which the Arles arena was originally put. There are traces among the stone terraces of what would have been the box reserved for the emperor and his entourage. It was the Roman emperors who were the primary promoters of the gladiatorial games, beginning with the very first emperor, Augustus, in the first century BC. His biographer Suetonius wrote that no one before Augustus 'had ever provided so many, so different, or such splendid public shows.' From now on these events became exercises in personal publicity conducted on the grandest possible scale. Invariably the most spectacular game held in arenas like those in Nîmes and Arles were associated with the imperial cult, with successive emperors straining to outdo their predecessors in the lavishness they bestowed on the games. It was a way of currying favour with the public by dazzling them with dramatic events all of which could be enjoyed free of charge.

There can be no doubt about the nature of their popular appeal. At the heart of these dramas in the open arena was the fight to the death. Today the only deliberate deaths witnessed in the Roman amphitheatres of Provence and Languedoc are during the seasonal *corridas*, the festivals of Spanish-style bullfighting which are still regularly held in both Nîmes and Arles, alongside the traditional local bull games, the *course libre*, in which the bull is not killed but merely taunted by agile young men whose purpose is to snatch a red *cocarde*, or rosette, that has been placed in just about the most dangerous place possible, on the bull's forehead right between its horns. It is the difference between a dangerous game and a ritual execution.

The *corrida* may be viewed as the last survivor of those Roman games in which death was the required final act. In the great amphitheatres of the Roman world, such as Arles and Nîmes, the event was known as the *munus*, and it would generally begin with a series of combats between wild animals. This was a sport to which the Romans were addicted, their leaders especially so. Fortunes were spent—and made—hunting down and capturing large animals from all parts of the empire, Africa above all. Surviving mosaics in museums throughout the

Combats with wild animals were a favourite spectator sport. The extensive Roman territories right across North Africa provided a lucrative trade in capturing tigers, lions and other wild creatures to satisfy the Romans' appetite for such contests.

Province illustrate some of the creatures that were most prized, the leopard being one of the favourites. According to Pliny the Elder, Julius Caesar at one time possessed no fewer than four hundred lions. His successor, Augustus, was not to be outdone. Over a period of fifteen years it has been calculated that 3,500 wild animals passed through his menagerie in Rome: these included six hundred leopards, four hundred tigers, two hundred and sixty lions, as well as an unknown quantity of elephants, bears, eagles, seals and a variety of smaller cats.

Watching these creatures fight and kill one another in combat was only one aspect of the Romans' favourite spectator sport. It had even darker aspects: the event would sometimes be spiced with 'punishment bouts' in which animals such as lions and leopards were released from trap-doors in the arena and set loose on unarmed criminals who might include prisoners of war, rebellious slaves, soldiers guilty of desertion or—during the later years of the Roman Empire—Christians. The persecution of Christians was never consistent under the empire. Yet under hard-line emperors, Diocletian prominent among them in the late fourth century, Christians were deemed to be as guilty as any other criminal by having refused to honour the official gods of the Roman state, particularly the emperor himself. This of course was unforgivable. Hence the Christians placed themselves outside the law of the land and deserved to be punished accordingly.

Yet all such combats—whether animals tearing one another apart or tearing Christians apart—were only the preliminaries. The main action in a Roman *munus* was the contest between two armed gladiators. This was the life-or-death contest the spectators had flocked in their thousands to see. The historian Livy, writing at the beginning of the first century AD, provides us with what little we know about the origins of these two-man combats, which seem to have begun as some kind of symbolic rite staged by a private sponsor in honour of a dead relative, the significance of which may be hard to grasp. But by the imperial era gladiatorial fights had become an impersonalised public spectacle organised on a vast scale. In the second century the Emperor Trajan is reputed to have celebrated a military victory by staging 10,000 gladiatorial combats over a period of 123 days: and even if this were a considerable exaggeration the scale of private sponsorship of such events still beggars belief.

Theatres and Amphitheatres

Gladiators were generally prisoners-of-war, captives from the Roman armies' numerous campaigns, whether in the Middle East, North Africa or against the Germanic tribes in Northern Europe. Those physically strong enough might be given the chance to train in hand-to-hand combat in special schools, sometimes for as long as two years, after which they would be hired as gladiators. The word means 'swordsman', and the sword was the gladiator's principal weapon, accompanied by a shield and protective helmet. His fifty-fifty chance of survival in each contest might not have seemed the most attractive odds, though preferable perhaps to the alternative which might well have been execution or at best an early death in the mines. Besides, the successful gladiator could receive handsome prize-money, and it is known that some even became quite wealthy. On the grimmer side, it was believed that few gladiators survived more than ten combats, or lived beyond the age of thirty.

The climax of every contest was the moment of death, or of the capitulation of one of the contestants. If the latter took place it was left to the sponsor to gauge the mood of the crowd as to whether the defeated fighter's plea for clemency should be accepted, or not. If rejected, the sponsor gave a thumbs-down signal, at which point the victorious gladiator delivered the *coup de grâce* with his sword plunged into the opponent's bared throat.

Even this final act was performed with ceremony. The Romans loved the theatricality of death, awarding it a high-minded significance as though it represented the ultimate triumph of manly virtue. Seneca, with his taste for heroic melodrama, expressed these sentiments perfectly: 'Death, when it is close to us, gives even to inexperienced men the courage to avoid the inevitable. So the gladiator, no matter how fainthearted he has been throughout the fight, offers his throat to his opponent and directs the wavering blade to the right spot.'

We have no record of whether Constantine, the first Christian emperor early in the fourth century, ever attended gladiatorial games. Arles being his favourite city he would have had every opportunity to visit the great amphitheatre, already two-and-a-half centuries old, to see for himself what his fellow Romans enjoyed as their preferred blood-sport. We do know that he strongly disapproved of these events, and on one occasion ordered 'that there shall be no more gladiatorial games'. His pronouncement appears to have been ignored, because games of some kind continued to take place in the arenas, even though there were no longer Christian martyrs being thrown to the lions. After all, since the games now offered no threat to the new official religion there seemed no good reason why they should not continue. It was not until early in the following century that the Christian hierarchy in Rome deemed that the games reeked too much of paganism; and as a result in the year 404 AD gladiatorial combats were finally banned.

The Romans clearly enjoyed other sports besides those involving slaughter in the arena. Chariot-racing was another favourite, possibly almost as much so as gladiatorial combats: but these events took place in large open hippodromes, or circuses, which in the Province and in Gaul generally have survived only in fragmentary ruins. They were never the massive stone structures like the amphitheatres which might have saved them from destruction. As it is they remain largely an image in the mind, created by elaborate oil-paintings of the kind which fed the romantic taste of nineteenth-century visitors to the Royal Academy in London and the Paris Salon—and more recently of course by Hollywood. For most of us Roman chariot-racing will be forever *Ben Hur*.

Survivors among Roman circuses in the Province today are modest in the extreme. Vienne possesses its curious 'needle', a kind of pyramid which is a third-century replacement for an obelisk which once graced the city's now-vanished hippodrome. In Arles the original obelisk dating from the first century AD, which formerly stood on the central island of a hippodrome more than four hundred feet in length, now rises elegantly in the city's main square, having been rescued from a private garden where it had served as an outsize stone bench. As for Nîmes, otherwise so rich in Roman monuments, all that remains of a circus once measuring five hundred feet in length is an insignificant slab of bare wall.

Monuments, and indeed buildings in general, can offer a distorted view of a society's way of life. And in this respect we may place too heavy an emphasis on surviving temples, theatres and amphitheatres, as though such places dominated the daily lives of those who lived here.

Theatres and Amphitheatres

A love of the natural world, and of hawking and hunting, are a feature of Roman decorative arts, particularly their mosaics and their stone-carving, as on this sarcophagus.

There were many popular Roman sports and pastimes which by their very nature required no buildings at all, and which are therefore in danger of being overlooked by those tempted to evaluate a past civilisation on the basis of what remains of it on the ground. A case in point is hunting. The Romans were passionate hunters. The possessive instinct which drew them into conquering much of the known world gave them a powerful appetite for capturing the wild creatures that inhabited those far regions. The records we have of the phenomenal number of beasts and birds they managed to obtain for sport in their arenas are eloquent proof of their prowess as huntsmen. Yet, to find evidence of that skill, that passion for the hunt, we can do no more than look at their decorative arts—their pottery, the vivid descriptive carvings on their sarcophagi and, above all, their mosaics which are so many miniature pictures of their world.

This is where the museums of the Province come into their own, typified by the handsome new museum of antiquities in Arles. In contrast to the mighty aqueducts straddling the landscapes, the triumphal arches standing proud on the edge of cities, and the temples, the theatres and amphitheatres, it is in the local museums such as the Musée de l'Arles Antique where so many intimate fragments of stone and ceramics can make you feel the pulse of Roman daily life—the warm human undercurrent flowing beneath the lordly monuments to Roman *gloria*. Here beside the statues of preening emperors and triumphant generals are the amphorae in which the wine and olive oil were stored, the mosaics of grape-picking and farmyard hens, the earthenware pots for ladies' perfumes and the bracelets and pendants given by some unnamed soldier to his wife.

In particular the Arles museum displays graceful carvings in low relief of girls dancing, their flowing robes delicately picked out with a sensitive touch. Love of the dance is not easily associated with a society impassioned by human blood-sports. But here is yet another debt to Greece, and to Greek sensibilities. And in a way it redeems the Romans. Not everything they enjoyed was Spartacus and Ben Hur.

10.
THE CHRISTIAN TAKEOVER

Provence, and the city of Arles in particular, lay at the heart of the dramatic conversion to Christianity which transformed the Roman Empire early in the fourth century. It was a transition that took place barely a decade after Christians had endured the most brutal persecution ever inflicted upon them, chiefly at the hands of a hysterical Emperor Diocletian. On the surface it seems as sudden and unexpected a turn of event as the conversion of Paul on the road to Damascus three centuries earlier. So, how on earth did it happen?

It is hard to obtain a sharp focus on the key events which led to such a historic milestone. The young Roman emperor, Constantine, in the long tradition of his forebears, was a brilliant soldier, and the son of a soldier. The role was virtually an imperative for a Roman leader: quite so extensive an empire, secured and maintained by force of arms, could scarcely have been ruled by a man lacking military experience. In fact, in the early years Constantine's authority extended to only half the empire, the region centred on the eastern Mediterranean being ruled by a certain Licinius, until Constantine eventually defeated him in battle to become sole emperor.

At what point in his life Constantine became a convert to Christianity is far from clear. But a mixture of popular legend and military events provides a useful guideline, pinpointing the year 312 AD as the seminal date when the course of history was changed. At that period Constantine was in Gaul, where the city of Arelate/Arles was his favourite residence. Without warning, his brother-in-law Maxentius took advantage of his absence from Rome by seizing power. Constantine promptly led an army into Italy to confront him. The decisive battle took place outside Rome, at Milvian Bridge, at which Maxentius' army was routed. Constantine became the unchallenged ruler of the western empire. Late in his life the emperor told his biographer Eusebius how on the long march to Rome he had experienced a vision in which a

The emperor who made the Roman Empire Christian, Constantine I. Arles was his favourite city.

The Christian Takeover

Christian sign appeared in the sky, with an accompanying message urging him to conquer his foe under this talisman. Another version of the story had Constantine order a Christian symbol to be painted on the shields of his troops before the battle.

Whatever actually took place during this Italian campaign, Constantine always attributed his success in this battle—and indeed all other military as well as political triumphs throughout his life—to his conversion to Christianity. How instant was that conversion it is impossible to know. It is recorded that two years earlier, when Constantine was still in Gaul, an orator spoke publicly of a vision which the emperor had received at a shrine of Apollo. It would not be far-fetched to imagine how the emperor's belief in a Christian god grew out of an adherence to the cult of Apollo: god of the sun, god of justice and in Greek mythology 'super-god'. It seems a plausible transition; Apollo, the son of Zeus, becomes Christ, son of the Christian god.

Constantine returned to Arles after his military triumph in Italy. Two years later, in the summer of 314, he summoned the bishops and other leading clergy from all over the Province and the western empire in general to attend an ecclesiastical conference in Arles. It was the first-ever international church council, and it placed Arles at the centre of the new Christian world of Western Europe. The bishops of York, Milan and Carthage were among those present; while local bishops included those of Marseille, Vienne and Vaison, as well as Arles itself.

It was an event without precedent, and must have been a bewildering experience for those assembled in Arles. Suddenly ecclesiastics old enough to remember fellow- Christians being thrown to the lions now found themselves lionised as leaders of the new official regime. Few turning-points in the history of Christianity have been as poignant as this.

Geographically Arles was ideally placed as the hub of this new Christian world. Whereas Rome was far away, Arles was the key link between Italy and Spain by means of the great highways stretching from the Alps to the Pyrenees; while the River Rhône provided an artery to central and northern Europe, as well as southwards to the flourishing ports of the western Mediterranean. Not surprisingly the city grew more prosperous and more important than ever. Under Constantine it became the administrative centre not only of the whole of

Roman Gaul, but of Spain, Britain and even parts of Germany, possessing its own treasury and minting its own imperial coins.

Landmarks of the city's finest hour survive. This was the period when the most celebrated Roman necropolis in the entire Province, Les Alyscamps, became transformed into the proudest of Christian burial-grounds; and when that most spectacular feat of Roman engineering, the aqueduct and water-mill of Barbégal, was in full production supplying the entire city with freshly-ground flour for its daily bread. But the most prominent legacy of Constantine's presence in Arles—if not exactly the most beautiful—is the complex of buildings in brick and stone known as the Baths of Constantine. These were public baths, set conveniently close to the river, and they were to be the last major building project in Roman Provence, originally larger even than the gigantic Baths of Caracalla in Rome. That they were constructed in the Christian era may seem irrelevant: yet the eye may detect a subtle link to what was to follow. The baths incorporate a semi-domed apse which foreshadows the apse to be found on some of the earliest Christian churches of the region. As ever, Roman engineering pointed the way ahead.

In hindsight, the story of the Christian Church before Constantine had not been entirely one of persecution. Not every Christian had been thrown to the lions. Within a few decades of Christ's death there were missionaries spread across much of the Roman world, obeying the proselytising instructions given by Jesus to his disciples. By the end of the first century a network of small Christian communities was in place, mainly in Greek territories but including a number in Latin Italy. Less than a century later flourishing Christian communities had grown up throughout the eastern Mediterranean, in Egypt and right across North Africa, as well as in Spain and Gaul, including of course the Province. Religious practice in these communities was disciplined and coherent. People shared a common faith, and a common routine of ritual and ceremony. They lived a structured life, and this structure was kept in place by a recognised hierarchy of bishops and lower clergy. They were also the ones who could read—principally Greek—and who therefore shared a

An area of the Baths of Constantine in Arles, with its semi-domed roof which became the model for the apse in early churches in the region.

familiarity with holy scriptures. We cannot know precisely what texts were available to such far-flung outposts, but they would almost certainly have been mainly in Greek, copies of texts relating to the life and teachings of Christ and the apostles, doubtless including many which would later become incorporated in the New Testament.

A distinguishing feature of these small communities is that they adhered to a strong and binding faith that was essentially simple—belief in a single all-powerful deity. Here was an all-embracing canopy under which to shelter. Such sharp focus was in contrast to the loose structure of the various pagan cults in the lands around them, with their multiplicity of gods adopting different forms and functions from place to place and season to season.

An even greater contrast was with the imperial cult imposed by successive Roman emperors on their subject peoples. It is hard to believe that a community imbued with the story of Christ and the Resurrection would be inclined to take seriously the deification of some strutting Roman warlord who had just commandeered the entire region and set up overblown statues of himself on every public building. The imperial cult may have spoken more of tyranny than of godliness. The priests in the community may even have been aware of Christ's words: 'Render therefore unto Caesar the things which are Caesar's, and unto God the things that are God's.'

The first of these Christian communities of any size in the Province was in the major city of Lugdunum (Lyon) early in the second century. This was barely a hundred years after the death of Christ: the missionaries spreading the gospel throughout the empire had done their work well. By the end of that century there were also substantial Christian communities further south along the Rhône Valley, in Vienne and, most conspicuously, in Arles. The city is known to have had its own bishop by the middle of the third century, a man by the name of Marcien, of whom there is no surviving trace, unlike the legendary 'first bishop', Trophimus, whose legacy is nothing less than Arles' magnificent mediaeval church and former cathedral, St. Trophime (see Chapter 8).

The question 'Why did Christianity win?' has tormented historians for centuries. One broad truth seems to be that right across Roman society, and in the minds of its subject people, a seismic change of heart took place during the course of the third century. A new vulnerability was gnawing at what for so long had been an unshakeable self-belief. To Romans in all walks of life the world they had created and relied upon no longer felt inviolate. There were political convulsions internally, with a rapid turnover of emperors. Further afield it was becoming increasingly hard to keep enemies at bay. Until the third century successive Roman emperors had successfully defended the empire's widely-spread borders; now a new alliance of hostile Germanic tribes had been formed in the north, while in the east there was an ever-growing Persian threat. The Roman armies, brilliantly trained though they might be might be, were sorely overstretched. The famous *Pax Romana* was beginning to feel a fragile thing. Inevitably these compounded upheavals brought about a steady economic decline. Trade suffered; travel was becoming more perilous. And on top of everything there were now severe outbreaks of the plague in Rome itself.

For a great many Romans it was the end of a rich and hedonistic way of life. Storm-clouds were gathering. On a personal level worship of the traditional gods was losing its appeal. When life had been good it had seemed natural to offer tokens of thanks to Jupiter and Apollo, and to bow to a ruling emperor and his deified predecessors. But now those official gods were seen to have let people down. And not surprisingly disenchanted citizens began increasingly to look for a source of authority elsewhere—to seek a form of faith which answered their growing doubts and fears, offering comfort and human understanding. In Christianity there was a religion founded on a ministry of love and healing, not glorification. Furthermore, in a world growing ugly it held out the promise of an afterlife in which virtue would be rewarded and wickedness punished. In short, whereas the gods of Rome touched only the face of life, the Christian god touched its soul.

So long as things had been going well the powers-that-be in Rome were unable to see it this way. Writers and historians remained just as hostile as their leaders. Pliny the Younger, often a sympathetic judge of human behaviour, wrote that to be a confessed Christian was punishable by death: but then he was also a senator at the time, and his letter was addressed to none other than the Emperor Trajan. Whatever his private view may have been, it would clearly have been suicide for a politician early in the second century to have expressed support for the Christian faith.

ROMAN PROVENCE

Pliny's close friend in Rome, the historian Tacitus, echoed what seems to have been the official view of the new religion. Christianity, he claimed, was 'a pernicious superstition' whose devotees were guilty of 'hatred of the human race'. Systematic persecution soon followed. The usual crime of which Christians were accused was their refusal to honour the official gods, and in particular to participate in the imperial cult. Suetonius, biographer of the first twelve Caesars, describes how in the early second century Christians were being punished for being 'a race of men given to a new and mischievous superstition'. All kinds of rumours were rife, many arising from church ceremonies, Holy Communion in particular. Resulting charges against Christians included arson, sexual perversion and (with obvious reference to the taking of bread and wine at Communion) cannibalism. Hysterical hatred was being born.

Persecution inevitably spread to the Province. In the reign of Marcus Aurelius late in the second century there was mass slaughter of Christians in Lyon, among the largest and earliest of Christian communities in the region. And from here violence spread to other communities in the Rhône Valley, Vienne, Valence, Orange, Avignon and Arles.

A surprising period of tolerance followed, greatly enhanced by a decree issued in the year 260 by the Emperor Gallienus. His motive may not have been entirely charitable: as a head of state desperately campaigning to secure the far borders of the empire he was naturally keen to avoid internal strife as well. As a result, in the decades that followed Christian communities multiplied and flourished in all the major cities in Italy and in the Province. No longer holding out in isolated pockets, Christians soon infiltrated all walks of Roman life. They had become an accepted power in the land.

Against a background, described earlier, of political instability and disenchantment at home, threats of invasion along the empire's borders, and economic decline generally, this might seem to have been the moment for the old gods to be pushed aside, and a fresh and more rigorous faith to take their place. Instead there was a violent conservative backlash. In 284AD, through the instruments of murder and civil war, Diocletian became Roman emperor of the west. His declared mission was to restore the greatness of Rome, and one of the means he chose for doing so was to promote what he perceived to be traditional Roman culture, rooted in its long-standing religious cults and the worship of the official gods of the Roman state. Hence there could be no more tolerance of Christians, who were now blamed (like Jews in Nazi Germany) for all the ills of the state. Within forty years of having been officially recognised, Christianity now became officially outlawed. Persecution on an unprecedented scale began in the first years of the fourth century, with a series of edicts each one more severe than the last. In the Province, as in Rome itself, churches were wrecked, sacred texts burnt, priests refusing to participate in the official state cults were tortured, beheaded, even burnt alive. The mildest punishment for a cleric was imprisonment. Christianity, literally and metaphorically, went underground.

In the east Christians fared just as badly. The eastern emperor, Galerius, was proud to persecute Christians with 'fire, cross and wild beasts', as he wrote chillingly. Galerius was a keen collector of lions, tigers and other carnivores, and was reputed to take a special delight in feeding Christians to them. One church leader in hiding described the emperor as 'an evil beast, quite unfit to rule'. An unexpected reprieve occurred when the emperor suffered a grave illness: fearing this might be a punishment meted out by the Christian god, in the year 311 he hurriedly issued an edict of tolerance—and then died.

It is hard to believe that these savage events took place barely three years before the western emperor, Constantine, summoned bishops from across the Roman Empire to attend the first international church council in Arles. For a church leader the transition from criminal to saviour had been bewilderingly rapid. Suddenly all those Christian institutions and disciplines which had taken root and flourished in the years of tolerance surfaced again and resumed their place now that the holocaust had passed.

It was a transition made the more puzzling to our eyes by the fact that Constantine's own father had actually served under Diocletian, both as a soldier and as a member of his government; and that Constantine himself, as a young soldier, had served under Galerius even while the emperor was feeding Christians to his lions and tigers. A particularly intriguing figure in these early years of the new Christian empire was Constantine's own indomitable mother, the Empress Helena. Converted to the Christian faith by her son, at the age of around eighty she set off for Jerusalem in search of traces of Jesus and his apostles. Besides founding churches in places associated with the life of Christ she succeeded in obtaining trophies by the cartload, most notably fragments of the Holy Cross, the nails included. Centuries later her horde of relics would satisfy the appetite of the mediaeval Church for objects supposedly related to Jesus and the saints. Helena's story lies far beyond the boundaries of this book, except that she was Constantine's mother, and her zeal and driving sense of purpose appear to typify the hold which the Christian story was capable of exerting on the Roman mind, and which the remote pantheon of Roman gods simply could not match. And if we should look for another reason why Christianity won, it may lie here.

By contrast to the grandiose monuments and colossal feats of engineering which mark the heyday of Roman Provence and Languedoc there is little to show for the early decades of Christianity in the region. At Riez, on the edge of the lavender fields north-east of Aix-en-Provence, stands a squat chunk of a building in the open landscape close to the remains of a Roman temple. This was an early-Christian baptistery erected on the site of a Roman holy spring—as ever the new god giving the old god a fresh face—and was once part of a long-vanished cathedral. Then, down on the coast, at Fréjus, the elegant remains of another early baptistery is preserved within the walls of the present Gothic cathedral. Like the Riez baptistery, this was constructed at least a century after the era of Constantine, only a short time before the final collapse of the Roman Empire.

The modesty of early church-building in the region matched the nature of early church leaders: perhaps, too, it was a reflection of so many years of repression and enforced secrecy. Christianity had survived in tight pockets. Now it was the turn of those pockets to unfold and expand. Here, as elsewhere in the Roman Empire, the spread of Christianity came about largely through the emergence of the great monasteries. And in Roman Provence the seeds of that expansion were sown along a stretch of what is now the Riviera coastline between Cannes and Marseille.

The Christian Takeover

One of the more shadowy figures in the story of the early Church was a hermit by the name of Honorat. Towards the end of the fourth century he found his place of solitude on a small island a short distance from an almost deserted area of rocky coastline more or less where Cannes is today. Honorat's reputation for piety soon attracted followers, and a small Christian settlement became established on the island. About the year 410 the settlement became a monastery, and within twenty years it supported a large community of monks, with a rare library of holy texts, and through lavish donations came to own extensive property on the mainland. And it was here, at the island monastery of St.-Honorat (as it was now called) that a man who was to become one of the key figures in the early Church—not only here in the Province but right across Western Europe—was first welcomed to this region. He was John Cassian, later to be revered as St. John Cassian.

The island of St.-Honorat is today one of the two inhabited Îles des Lérins, and a Cistercian monastery remains, though nothing of the original abbey survives. But its most distinguished visitor, John Cassian, who was received here about the year 415, has left a rich and tantalising legacy, not here at St. Honorat but further west along the coast in the former Greek port of Massalia, now Marseille, where he decided to settle.

Cassian was born in the eastern empire, probably in what is now Romania, about the year 360. In circumstances largely unknown to us he became drawn to the mystical life of the Christian desert fathers, most notably St. Jerome whom he may well have known. Cassian travelled to Palestine and then to Egypt. After many years he made his way to the capital of the eastern empire, Constantinople, where he became ordained; then in 404 he travelled to Rome. Here the pope invited him to found an Egyptian-style monastery in southern Gaul, and Cassian duly arrived in the Province, where he was welcomed at the newly-founded monastery of St.-Honorat and then by the Christian community in Massalia.

It was here in Marseille that he set about founding the abbey which was to become the most powerful Christian institution in the entire Province, eventually spawning no fewer than three hundred further monasteries and priories in the region. This was the great abbey of St.-Victor. The abbey itself no longer exists, and the abbey church was vastly rebuilt in the thirteenth century, yet an important fragment of the original church—its crypt—does survive.

Marseille: the Abbey Church of St.-Victor

The crypt of the abbey church of St.-Victor in Marseille, and the grotto which leads off it, together lie at the very roots of early Christian life in the final century of Roman rule in southern Gaul. In this underground labyrinth history and legend are intertwined: legend takes off where history ends, while history itself is richly coloured by legend. The cavernous low-vaulted crypt contains the fifth-century sarcophagus of Cassian himself, who died here in 435. He had devoted the last twenty years of his life to theological writings which are said to have been much admired by St. Benedict, father of the Benedictine Order at Monte Cassino a century later and author of a historic code of discipline for monks, known as the Rule of St. Benedict. Hence Cassian can be described, along with his slightly older contemporaries, St. Jerome and St. Augustine, as one of the spiritual founders of western monasticism.

The monasteries which were Cassian's most tangible legacy in Roman Provence have long since vanished or been superseded. Physically there survives only his tomb, and the crypt of his original abbey

A shrine to a Christian legend: the grotto beneath the abbey church of St.-Victor in Marseille, with the 'altar of Mary Magdalene' and the primitive carved head (right) known as the 'pillar of Lazarus'.

The Christian Takeover

Sarcophagus said to contain the body of John Cassian, founder of St.-Victor, the earliest abbey in Roman Provence.

church. St. Victor, to whom the abbey was dedicated, was an early Christian martyr who met his end through one of those diabolical punishments so relished by hagiographers, being crushed to death between two millstones (and so, by a morbid twist, becoming the patron saint of millers). By repute his tomb is deeply buried within the rock of the accompanying grotto. Its possible whereabouts is signalled by a free-standing column supporting the rock-ceiling, with a primitive carved head cut into the capital. At some stage, we do not know precisely when, this became known as the head of Lazarus, the friend of Jesus whom Christ brought back from the dead. Furthermore, set into the rock-face close by, are the remains of a plain stone altar (surmounted now by a seventeenth-century carved panel): and this too has long carried a biblical association. It is known as the altar of Mary Magdalene.

We are now leaping into legend. These twin associations with biblical figures allude to a local story which in centuries to come was to inspire and divide the Christian world, and has continued to seduce romantic imaginations ever since. This is the legend of Mary Magdalene and her miraculous voyage on a raft from the Holy Land to these shores in the company of her brother Lazarus together with members of Christ's family.

ROMAN PROVENCE

It is impossible to know when the grotto of St. Victor became associated with this legend: historians have generally agreed that it would have been long after the period of Roman rule. None the less the legend itself is rooted here in the ancient city of Massalia during the Roman era. Its setting is in the very place where John Cassian chose to found his first abbey. Here, next to where he built the crypt, is the grotto where, as the story goes, Mary Magdalene and her brother Lazarus took refuge after their journey from the Holy Land. The grotto would certainly have been used as a Christian sanctuary during the centuries of persecution, which may be why Cassian chose the site. It was already a sacred place. There is also evidence, explained in the Postscript, that a story of biblical figures from the circle of Christ arriving miraculously at these shores on a raft may already have been circulating in Roman Provence, and been known to Cassian: hence an even stronger reason for establishing his first abbey here. As for the specific association with Mary Magdalene, this may well have been made a good deal later, once the romanticized cult of the Magdalene had begun to take hold of the imagination of pilgrims and churchmen in general early in the ninth century. Whatever the truth, the crypt and grotto of St. Victor are the cradle of one of the most fertile of all Christian legends.

Fewer than fifty years separate the death of John Cassian from the ending of all Roman rule in the Province. The final collapse was relatively sudden. For centuries successive Roman emperors had contained the threat of Germanic tribes, holding the River Rhine as a natural barrier. Then from the third century that threat grew increasing intense. Saxon, Frankish and Gothic tribes, traditionally in conflict with each other as much as with the Romans, formed a loose confederation enabling their combined armies to mount effective strikes to the west of the Rhine, creating widespread chaos and disruption in Roman Gaul.

For more than a century the invasions affected the more northerly regions, and the Province itself remained largely unaffected. The Christianisation initiated by the Emperor Constantine proceeded. Churches and abbeys were established. But then, at the beginning of the fifth century, a tidal wave of invaders broke over southern Europe, from the

The Christian Takeover

Balkans in the east to Gaul and Spain in the west. In 410 Rome itself was sacked by Alaric. At much the same time a huge band of Visigoths—seemingly an entire tribe—crossed the Rhine and began to sweep west and southwards across Gaul. The overstretched Roman armies were helpless. By the year 413 the Visigoths had advanced into the northern part of the Province, overwhelming the key city of Lugdunum, then pressing on down the Rhône Valley. Further west the Germanic armies streamed through what is now Aquitaine. Again the Roman legions were powerless. By 418—humiliatingly—the Roman emperor felt compelled to accept a truce in return for recognising an independent Visigothic kingdom within a crumbling Roman Empire, with its capital at Tolosa (Toulouse).

The Province was now virtually surrounded. For a while, in the south and east of the region, Marseille and the towns along the coast towards Italy seem to have remained unaffected, this being precisely the time when John Cassian was establishing his abbeys and priories. Besides, the Visigoths, having converted to Christianity by this time, would not have presented any religious threat to the emerging Church. But politically the status quo was not to last long. By the third quarter of the fifth century virtually the whole of the Province, including Marseille, was in the hands of the Visigoths. And in the spring of 468, after a siege lasting eighteen months, Arles, by now among the most important cities in Western Europe, became the last Roman stronghold to fall. As a final humiliation, in 475 the emperor formally agreed to surrender the region to the Visigothic King Euric.

And so Roman rule in Gaul ended where it had begun six hundred years earlier—in Provence. And two years later Rome's entire western empire ceased to exist.

Albrecht Dürer's imposing 1512 portrait of Emperor Charlemagne

Postscript:
After the Romans

The Visigoths put an end to 600 years of Roman rule in Provence and Languedoc. It was a dramatic *finale* brought about, just as it had begun, by military conquest. Yet it turned out to be something of an anticlimax, for within thirty years the Visigoths had themselves been driven out of the region and into Spain by an even more powerful Germanic tribe, the Franks.

Not surprisingly the Visigoths left no conspicuous imprint on the Province during their brief stay. The Franks, on the other hand, remained long enough to bequeath their name to the entire territory that had once been Roman Gaul, causing it to be known ever after as 'France'. The Franks established what became known as the Merovingian dynasty, which continued to rule the former Roman Province for the next two centuries. A number of the early churches in the region date from this era, among them the elegant Merovingian baptistery in the fortified hill-town of Venasque. But the most notable legacy of the Franks was due to a rival Frankish tribe which replaced the Merovingians in the eighth century. This was the Carolingian dynasty, whose greatest leader was the Emperor Charlemagne. And it was in Charlemagne's hands that history seemed to turn full-circle, because his most enduring triumph was to re-create the former Roman Empire, now with the pope its spiritual leader, as the *Holy* Roman Empire.

In a sense, then, the Roman Empire lived on—just as, in the region that was once Julius Caesar's 'Province of Rome', its grandiose monuments still live on: the theatres and amphitheatres, the vast network of roads, the towers and ramparts, temples and triumphal arches, and above all those astonishing feats of engineering, the aqueducts, which still crisscross the unchanging Provençal landscape.

The rediscovery and rehabilitation of this Roman landscape was to a large extent a product of French nineteenth-century Romanticism. French art-lovers frequenting the annual Paris Salon had long been relishing picturesque scenes of rustic life enacted in the theatrical setting of Roman ruins. Now, with wars and revolutions temporarily in abeyance, and travel made easier with the arrival of the steam-train, sophisticated Parisians with a taste for the classical world wanted to see those Roman monuments for themselves. Hence this became the era of the great restoration programmes initiated by Prosper Mérimée in his official capacity as Chief Inspector of Ancient Monuments.

At the same time that Mérimée was tidying up the Roman monuments of Provence and Languedoc another strain of French Romanticism was embracing the region's classical past, and incorporating it into a celebration of traditional Provençal culture. This was the group of local poets who called themselves the *Félibrige*, and who wrote only—and defiantly—in the Provençal language rather than in French. Their founder (and future Nobel Prize-winner) was Frédéric Mistral; and not long after the Arles amphitheatre had been cleared of mediaeval dwellings it was here that Gounod's opera based on Mistral's most famous work, *Mirèio*, was performed. Thereafter the Roman theatres and amphitheatres of this region became the natural setting for public entertainment of all kinds, from bull-fights and arts festivals to jazz concerts and operatic productions. The spirit of those pleasure-loving Romans was reborn.

Then there is the legacy of legend. One in particular has proved to be as durable as the Roman monuments themselves, and it belongs intimately to this region. It is easy to imagine how the new faith would have hungered for links with the Holy Land in which it was rooted. And that link came in the form of a legend of a tiny raft which almost literally brought the Holy Land to Provence.

This is the legend of the three Marys, one of whom was Mary Magdalene, and their arrival in Roman Provence shortly after the Resurrection of Christ to which Mary Magdalene had been a witness. It was her closeness to the central event in the Christian story which accounts for the supreme importance awarded the Magdalene in the eyes of the early Church. For a newly-converted Christian land, so distant in time and place from events described in the New Testament, she brought first-hand contact with Christ himself and His message to the world. She was seen as His messenger. And here she was in this land, where she lived for the rest of her life—so people were led to believe. Other occupants of the legendary raft included Mary Salome, mother of the apostles James and John, Mary Jacob, sister of the Virgin Mary, the Magdalene's brother Lazarus whom Christ had brought back from the dead, and her sister Martha. Altogether it was a glorious pantheon of biblical saints.

No wonder this story, particularly as it related to Mary Magdalene, made an impact which was to reverberate for centuries, responsible for some of the most supreme art and architecture in Europe, as well as displays of deceit and skulduggery on a scale rarely equalled in the history of the Christian Church. And, as is so often the case, the two are wellnigh inseparable.

In the crypt of the abbey church of St.-Maximin, to the east of Aix-en-Provence, are a number of ancient tombs which have lain there since Roman times, dating from the beginning of the Christian era. Here it was long believed lay the body of Mary Magdalene. The belief was not entirely fanciful. The abbey bore the name of its supposed founder, Maximin, who had been a disciple of Jesus, and one of the biblical figures believed to have arrived here in Provence on the legendary raft from the Holy Land. Here Maximin was said to have founded the first abbey. Meanwhile Mary Magdalene spent thirty years as a hermit in a cave in the nearby hills. On her death Maximin had her buried in the abbey, and later was himself buried there.

But there was another story. Claims were made by an abbey in Burgundy that at the time of the Saracen invasions Mary Magdalene's relics were removed for safety—in fact stolen—from St.-Maximin and taken to the new abbey of Vézelay. Relics of the saints and those close to Jesus were a powerful focus of Christian faith in mediaeval Europe, and to have obtained such things was to be in possession of a golden treasury. The most conspicuous outcome of Vézelay's claim was that the abbey became immensely wealthy. Pilgrims, rich and poor, flocked there in their thousands, and donations poured in. It soon became the most famous shrine in France.

In the year 1279 the count of Provence, Charles of Anjou, brother of the King of France, decided that enough was enough and the honour of Provence needed to be restored. He took himself to St.-Maximin determined to conduct a thorough investigation of the tombs in the abbey church. Four ancient sarcophagi lay in the crypt. And Count Charles set to work. It was said that he toiled with his bare hands to remove the dirt of centuries and reveal the contents of the tombs. Soon he was richly rewarded. One of the tombs was found to contain a body which was said to have emitted a 'sweet odour'. It was accompanied, so it was claimed, by an inscription verifying the identity of the body as being that of Mary Magdalene, as well as accounting for its presence here. A twist in the story was added by the count's spokesmen, explaining that the saint's remains had long ago been placed in one of the adjacent tombs, apparently to foil Saracen raids. Instead, what it actually did was to foil the thief sent specially by the Burgundian abbey. In other words Vézelay had managed to steal the wrong body.

In fact, the document reputed to have been found in the tomb, if it ever existed at all, was undoubtedly a forgery, just as all the documents which had been claimed as proof of ownership by Vézelay had also been forged, probably by the abbey's zealous scribes.

None the less, by papal pronouncement St.-Maximin became the acknowledged guardian of the body of Mary Magdalene. The reputation of Vézelay as a place of international pilgrimage simply shrivelled away. The Burgundian abbey church became, as it has remained to this day, the largest and most magnificent parish church in France. It is the great church on the hill.

As for St.-Maximin, Count Charles built a new church and monastery over the crypt, installing Dominican friars who also became custodians of the forest cave nearby, at Ste.-Baume, where the saint was reputed to have lived as a hermit until her death, and which soon became a focus of pilgrimage, as it still is, on a scale approaching that of Vézelay in its years of pomp.

The legend of a miraculous raft bringing followers of Jesus to Provence from the Holy Land may well have been circulating as early as Roman times. We know that on the coast in the heart of the Camargue marshlands a church was established in the fourth century on the site of a Roman temple, and that in the sixth century the Bishop of Arles

Postscript: After the Romans

The scarred façade of the abbey church at St. Maximin, built over the supposed tomb of Mary Magdalene. One of the oldest legends in Provence tells of the saint's arrival on these shores from the Holy Land after the Crucifixion and Resurrection of Christ.

described this church as carrying the dedication to 'Sainte-Marie-de-Ratis'—St. Mary of the Raft. Since there is no indication that this was a new dedication it seems likely that the church had always been associated with the legend of the raft and the saints from the sea. It may even be why the church was founded, probably during the reign of Constantine at the time when the emperor was living in his favourite city, Arles, not far away. Which particular Mary the church was first dedicated to is not known, only that at some future date there were claimed to be three Marys on that raft, one of them being Mary Magdalene. Out of these hopeful dreams one of the most captivating of Christian legends was born.

Today manifestations of that legend live on, though without the profiteering mendacity exercised by rulers and Church leaders in the Middle Ages. Instead there is charm, and there is theatre. In Marseille, close to the abbey church of St. Victor founded by John Cassian in the fifth century, stands the oldest bakery in the city, called the Four des

ROMAN PROVENCE

A sea-legend commemorated: in the mediaeval church of Les Saintes-Maries-de-la-Mer a miniature vessel holds effigies of two of the biblical Marys said to have arrived here from the Holy Land to found the very first church in Roman Provence.

Navettes. Its speciality is a small pastry—a *navette*—in the shape of a boat; and on 2 February each year the fishermen of Marseille form a procession along the Old Port to St.-Victor for Candlemass where *navettes* are sold and handed out. The ceremony is in celebration of that same legend of Mary Magdalene and her companions arriving on these shores by sea. Perhaps for culinary reasons the raft is more conveniently represented by a boat, and it is flavoured with rose-water, appropriately enough since it emits the 'sweet odour' which was said to have accompanied the Magdalene's remains all those centuries ago. If Count Charles were able to be present he would doubtless recognise the odour.

Then there is the more dramatic legacy in the small coastal town in the Camargue named after those saints from the sea, Les Saintes-Maries-de-la-Mer. Here, in the church built on the site of the original St. Mary of the Raft, an evocative and touching ceremony takes place each year on 25 May, when effigies of two of the Marys, in a small painted boat, are carried in a formal procession from the church to the seashore. They are Mary Salome and Mary Jacob, the two who stayed behind after Mary Magdalene departed for St.-Maximin and her her-

Postscript: After the Romans

mitage. And here at the water's edge the toy boat with its miniature figures is lowered until it appears to be floating on the sea, just as in legend the raft carrying them had floated here, bringing Christianity to these pagan lands. The scene has the innocent charm of a Christmas crib or a school nativity play.

The legacy of the Romans in Provence is rich and varied, wherever we look. A toy boat floating on the sea feels a long way from amphitheatres and striding aqueducts. The essential link is the church. The Saintes-Maries church, guardian of the sea legend, is a gaunt hulk rising amid the old town and crowned with battlements, redolent of violent times. It dates from the Middle Ages, a time when Christianity was resurgent after centuries of instability and invasion. This was the era when the great cathedrals and abbeys of Europe were being created, and when the Benedictine monk and chronicler from Cluny, Raoul Glaber, could write so movingly, 'Even the little churches in the villages were reconstructed by the faithful more beautiful than before.' He added with his often-quoted lyrical observation: 'One would have said that the world itself was casting aside its old age and clothing itself anew in a white mantle of churches.'

These new churches, hundreds of thousands of them right across the continent of Europe, were being built in the style we know as 'Romanesque'. In other words they were inspired by Roman architecture, with its rounded arches, its load-bearing stone columns and echoing vaulted spaces—except that now those engineering feats were being practised for quite a new purpose. The Romans had by and large employed their formidable building skills for material ends, for people's daily needs and pleasures. Now those same skills were being harnessed for people's spiritual needs. A muscular, resurgent Church needed places of worship that were capable of expressing the new energy and self-confidence of the Christian faith. So the church-builders turned to the Romans.

Hence the natural heirs of the great amphitheatres and triumphal arches, the giant thermal baths, the Pont du Gard and those long-striding aqueducts, were the new cathedrals and abbeys of Europe, and especially that 'white mantle of churches' which were now covering the land. Here was Roman genius reborn, and perhaps its finest legacy of all.

Further Reading

Local bookshops in the region, particularly those attached to Roman sites, stock a variety of well-illustrated guidebooks in several languages, which by and large I have found to be well-researched and extremely useful. For those who wish to dig deeper into the Roman past in Provence and Languedoc here is a list of other publications which have been helpful to me, though they are less likely to be picked up in local bookshops.

Auguet, Roland, *Cruelty and Civilisation: the Roman Games*. London: 1972
Benko, Stephen (ed.), *Early Church History: the Roman Empire and the Setting of Primitive Christianity*. London: 1972
Bromwich, James, *The Roman Remains of Southern France*. London: 1993
Caesar, Julius, *War Commentaries: de bello Gallico*. London: 1965
Cook, Theodore, *Old Provence*. (1905) Oxford: 2000
Drinkwater, J. F., *Roman Gaul, the Three Provinces*. Ithaca, NY: 1983
Durrell, Lawrence, *Caesar's Vast Ghost*. London: 1990
Everitt, Anthony, *The First Emperor, Caesar Augustus and the Triumph of Rome*. London: 2006
Garland, Robert, *Julius Caesar*. Bristol: 2004
Goldsworthy, Adrian, *Caesar, the Life of a Colossus*. London: 2006
Hackett, Olwen, *Roman Gaul*. London: 1953
Hamey, L. A., *The Roman Engineers*. Cambridge: 1981
Hatt, Jean-Jacques, *Celts and Gallo-Romans*. London: 1970
Hodge, Alfred, *Roman Aqueducts and Water Supply*. London: 1992
Hopkins, Keith, *A World Full of Gods: Pagans, Jews and Christians in the Roman Empire*. London: 1999
Johnson, Hugh, *The Story of Wine*. London: 1989
Jones, Arnold, *Augustus*. London: 1970
Kee, Alistair, *Constantine versus Christ: the Triumph of Ideology*. London: 1982
Kyle, Donald G., *Spectacles of Death in Ancient Rome*. London: 1998

Further Reading

MacKendrick, Paul, *Roman France*. (London: 1971
Mullins, Edwin, *The Camargue, Portrait of a Wilderness*. Oxford: 2009
Murphy, Trevor, *Pliny the Elder's Natural History*. Oxford: 2004
O'Connor, Colin, *Roman Bridges*. Cambridge: 1993
Odahl, Charles, *Constantine and the Christian Empire*. London: 2004
Pope-Hennessy, James, *Aspects of Provence*. London: 1965
Rivet, Albert, *Gallia Narbonensis*. London: 1988
Sear, Frank, *Roman Theatres*. Oxford: 2006
Stamper, John, *The Architecture of Roman Temples*. Cambridge: 2005
Stewart, Columba, *Cassian the Monk*. Oxford: 1998
Suetonius, *The Twelve Caesars*. London: 1989
Thomas, Edmund, *Monumentality and the Roman Empire*. Oxford: 2007
Welch, Kathleen, *The Roman Amphitheatre*. Cambridge: 2007
White, Kenneth, *Roman Farming*. London: 1970
Woolf, Greg, *Becoming Roman: the Origins of Provincial Civilisation in Gaul*. Cambridge: 1998

Selected Museums & Visitor Centres

Virtually every town and large village in the region possesses a museum of some sort, often with a display of antiquities consisting of a Roman amphora, a broken scent-bottle and half-a-dozen coins. Here is a short-list of museums and visitor centres which display a great deal more.

Aix-en-Provence: Musée Granet (http://www.museegranet-aixenprovence.fr)
Ambrussum: Archaeological museum in preparation
Antibes: Musée d'Archéologie (http://www.antibes-juanlespins.com/fr/culture/musees)
Apt: Musée d'Histoire et d'Archéologie du Pays d'Apt (http://www.vaucluse.fr/597-le-musee-d-histoire-et-d-archeologie-du-pays-d-apt.htm)
Arles: Musée de l'Arles Antique (http://www.arles-antique.cg13.fr)
Avignon: Musée Lapidaire (http://www.avignon.fr/fr/culture/musees/lapidaire.php)
Camargue: Musée Camarguais (http://www.avignon-et-provence.com/musees/musee-camargue)
Cannes (Île Sainte-Marguerite): Musée de la Mer (http://www.cannes.com)
Fréjus: Musée Archéologique Municipal de Fréjus (http://www.visitvar.fr)
La Turbie: Musée du Trophée des Alpes (http://www.ville-la-turbie.fr)
Marseille: Musée d'Histoire de Marseille (http://www.marseille.fr)
    Musée des Docks Romains (http://www.marseille.fr)
    Jardin des Vestiges Jardin (http://www.marseille.fr)
Nice: Musée et Site Archéologique Nice-Cemenulum (http://www.musee-archeologique-nice.org)
Nîmes: Musée Archeologique de Nîmes (http://www.nimes.fr)
   " : Arènes de Nîmes, Maison Carrée – Tour Magne (http://www.arenes-nimes.com)
Orange: Musée d'Art et d'Histoire d'Orange (http://www.theatre-antique.com/orange/526-le_musee_d_orange)
Pont du Gard (http://www.pontdugard.fr)

Museums

St,-Rémy de Provence: Musée Archéologique, Hôtel de Sade (http://www.saintremy-de-provence.com)
Site Archéologique de Glanum (http://glanum.monuments-nationaux.fr)
Vaison-la-Romaine: Musée Archéologique Théo Desplans (http://www.vaison-la-romaine.com)
Vienne: Musée des Beaux-Arts et d'Archéologie (http://www.vienne.fr)

INDEX

Agrippa, Marcus Vipsanius 40, 42, 50, 63, 64, 91, 104, 127
Ahenobarbus, Domitius 4, 20, 24, 113
Aix-en-Provence 3, 5, 11, 85, 91, 123
Allobroges 3, 4, 19, 20, 22
Alpilles 9, 11, 13, 16, 52, 64, 66, 82
Ambrones 8
Ambrussum 99, 100, 106, 108, 109
   Pont Ambroix 106-107
Antibes 116
Apt 40, 111
Apta Julia, *see* Apt
Aquae Sextiae, *see* Aix-en-Provence
Arausio, *see* Orange
Arc, River 11, 12
Arelate, *see* Arles
Arles 9, 23, 24, 25, 26, 28, 39, 43, 64, 71, 82, 83, 88, 89, 90, 110, 133, 139, 144, 145, 146, 150, 151, 153, 155
   Amphitheatre 145, 146
   Les Alyscamps 133, 134, 156
   Musée de l'Arles Antique 82, 90, 110, 139, 151
   St.-Trophime 46, 133, 158
Aurelius, Marcus 37
Ausonius 89
Avignon 3, 9, 74, 110
   Musée Lapidaire 74

Baeterrae, *see* Béziers
Barbégal watermill 81-84, 88, 156
Beaucaire 8, 110
Béziers, 25, 71, 105
Brutus, Decimus 24

Cabellio, *see* Cavaillon
Caesar, Augustus 28, 29, 30, 31, 32, 34, 36, 37, 39, 40, 42, 46, 50, 56, 63, 64, 67, 69, 77, 85, 87, 88, 119, 122, 126, 127, 135, 136, 137, 146
Caesar, Julius 1, 4, 18, 19, 20, 21, 22, 23, 24, 25, 26, 28, 37, 50, 57, 77, 88, 89, 90, 148
Caius Sextius Calvinus 3

Caligula, Emperor 37, 64, 137
Camargue 9, 25, 78, 79, 80, 113, 172
   Musée de la Camargue 80
Camars, Aulus Annius 80
Carpentras 41, 42
Carthage 1
Cato, Marcus Porcius 75
Caumont 76
Cavaillon 3, 41, 111
Celts 3, 5, 17, 20, 21, 31, 42, 51, 129, 131
Cemenulem, *see* Cimiez
Ceyreste 67
Charlemagne, Holy Roman Emperor 169
Charles of Anjou 171, 172
Christianity 153, 154, 155, 156, 158, 159, 160, 161
Cimbri 6, 7
Cimiez 93, 94, 116, 144
Claudius, Emperor 37, 96, 122, 137
Cleopatra 29, 30, 40, 63, 91
Constantine, Emperor 138, 149, 150, 153, 154, 155, 156, 161, 166
Cook, Sir Theodore 58, 68
Coulon, River 111, 112, 113
Courbet, Gustave 107
Crassus 23, 24
Cyrus the Great 1, 11

Die 42
Dio, Cassius 34
Diocletuian, Emperor 153, 160, 161
Domitian, Emperor 96
Durance, River 41, 74, 76, 89, 111, 113, 114, 115
Durrell, Lawrence 58, 63, 134

Entremont 3, 17, 85
Etang de Berre 77

Forcalquier 114
Formigé, Jules 142
Forum Julii, *see* Fréjus
Fos-sur-Mer 8, 24, 55

Index

Franks 169
Fréjus 25, 30, 31, 39, 43, 67, 116, 144, 162
  Aqueduct 67, 68
  Lanterne d'Auguste 31

Galerius, Emperor 161
Gallienus, Emperor 160
Gardon, River 58
Gauguin, Paul 133, 134
Gaul 2, 4, 5, 6, 7, 8, 11, 12, 18, 19, 20, 21, 22, 25, 26, 28, 30, 32, 39, 42, 43, 46, 50, 55, 69, 71, 72, 73, 80, 83, 85, 86, 87, 89, 91, 99, 103, 105, 109, 121, 143, 153
Gallia Narbonnensis 5, 30
Gier aqueduct 65, 66
Gladiators 146, 147, 148, 149
Glanum 16, 17, 18, 19, 46, 48, 49, 50, 51, 66, 77, 94, 111, 130, 131

Hadrian, Emperor 37, 40, 91, 96, 140
Hannibal 2, 4, 6, 9, 110
Hérault, River 105
Hyères 116

Julia, wife of Caius Marius 14, 18, 20
Justinius 71

La Ciotat 67
La Garde-Adhémar 130
La Turbie 34, 35, 36, 116
Lazarus 13, 165, 171
Les Baux-de-Provence 13
Le Tholonet 66
Ligurians 3
Livia, wife of Augustus 122
Livy 144, 148
Lugdunum, *see* Lyon
Lyon 5, 65, 73, 89, 97, 158

Maecenas, Gaius 63
Marcus Aurelius, Emperor 160
Mark Antony 29, 30, 31, 40, 63, 91
Marius, Caius (or Gaius) 7, 8, 9, 10, 11, 12, 13, 16, 18, 19, 20, 55, 56
Marseille 1, 2, 3, 17, 19, 23, 24, 48, 71, 77, 85, 86, 163, 174
  Abbey Church of St.-Victor 164-166
  Musée des Docks Romains 77
Martha Magdalene 14, 171
Martha, prophetess 10, 13, 16
Martial 69, 91
Mary Jacob 171
Mary Magdalene 14, 165, 170, 174
Mary Salome 171
Mas des Tourelles 74, 75, 76
Massalia, *see* Marseille
Matisse, Henri 94
Maxentius 153
Menton 35
Mérimée, Prosper 123, 142, 170
Mistral, Frédéric 88, 170
Mont (Montagne) Ste.-Victoire 12, 16, 66

Narbo, *see* Narbonne
Narbonne 5, 25, 30, 43, 71, 91, 105
Nemausus, *see* Nîmes
Nero, Emperor 37, 137
Nîmes 31, 39, 40, 43, 61, 62, 63, 64, 67, 71, 79, 86, 91, 92, 93, 109, 125, 126, 127, 128, 129, 144, 145, 150
  Amphitheatre 144, 145
  Carré d'Art 129
  Castellum Divisorium 62
  Jardins de la Fontaine 93, 132
  Maison Carrée 91, 125-129
  Temple of Diana 132
  Tour Magne 32, 33, 39, 93, 132

Orange 42, 43, 110, 135, 137, 140, 141, 142, 143
  Theatre 140-143
  Triumphal Arch 43-44
Ouvèze, River 115, 116

Peccaïs 79
Peccaius 79
Pius, Antoninus 37, 38, 91
Pliny the Elder 34, 69, 72, 73, 74, 75, 80, 144, 148
Pliny the Younger 72, 159
Plutarch 8, 9, 10, 11, 12, 22, 30, 69

181

ROMAN PROVENCE

Pompey 23, 24, 25, 89, 90
Pont de Ganagobie 114, 116
Pont de Tuve 116
Pont du Gard 57-64, 92, 108, 119
Pont Flavien 116, 118, 119
Pont Julien 111-115
Pourrières 12, 18, 19, 20
Provincia (Roman Provence) 1, 5, 20, 23, 25, 26, 29, 30, 31, 31, 34, 36, 37, 67, 71, 103, 122
Pyrenees 2, 4

Rhône, River 1, 8, 9, 23, 39, 42, 64, 74, 79, 80, 98, 109, 155
Riez 124, 125, 162
Roman gods 121, 124, 131, 155
Rome 1, 2, 3, 6, 55, 143, 156

St.-Blaise 78
St.-Cyr-sur-Mer 95
St.-Honorat (Îles des Lérins) 163
St. John Cassian 163, 164, 166
St.-Maximin 171, 172, 174
St.-Rémy de Provence 3, 16, 45, 46, 111
  Les Antiques 45-52
St.-Romain-en-Gal 98, 99
St.-Thibéry bridge 107
Ste.-Baume 172
Saintes-Maries-de-la-Mer, Les 174, 175
Sallust 7, 56
Salon-de-Provence 123
Salt 78, 79
Salyens 3, 16, 19, 20, 78
Segustero, *see* Sisteron
Seneca 130, 135, 136
Segovia 54
Sisteron 114
Slavery 3, 20, 44, 47, 63, 67, 69, 71, 73, 74, 80, 92, 109, 143, 148
Smollett, Tobias 58
Spain 2, 4, 7, 8, 23, 30, 32, 39, 50, 76, 89, 99, 103, 110, 116, 155
Stendhal 58
Strabo 69, 111
Suetonius, Gaius 22, 23, 28, 29, 45, 63, 135, 146
Tacitus 30, 45, 72, 160

Teutones 6, 7, 8, 9, 11, 12, 18, 104
Tiberius, Emperor 37, 44, 45, 127, 137
Trajan, Emperor 37, 148, 159
Tremaïe, Les 13-16
Trophée des Alpes 34-36, 93

Ugernum, *see* Beaucaire
Uzès 61, 92

Vaison-la-Romaine 95, 96, 116, 139
Valence 110
Van Gogh, Vincent 46, 88, 133, 134
Vasio, *see* Vaison-la-Romaine
Venasque 169
Vercingetorix 21, 22
Vernègues 124
Vézelay 171, 172
Via Appia 55
Via Agrippa 42, 43, 89, 104, 110, 115, 116
Via Aurelia 25, 32, 89, 103, 104, 110, 116, 133
Via Domitia 4, 24, 32, 89, 103, 105, 106, 109, 110, 111, 113, 114, 115, 116
Vienna, *see* Vienne
Vienne 19, 22, 42, 65, 71, 97, 98, 99, 122, 123, 137, 138
  Plan de l'Aiguille 22
  Temple 122, 123
Visigoths 167, 169
Vitruvius, Marcus 56, 57, 60, 97, 107, 145

Wine 71, 73, 74